TEAM+WORK =SUCCESS

The Formula That Is the Solution

Dennis Reilly

Disclaimer: The recommendations, advice, descriptions, and methods in this book are presented solely for educational purposes. The author and publisher assume no liability whatsoever for any loss or damage that results from the use of any of the materials in this book. Use of the material in this book is solely at the risk of the user.

Published by The Firefighter Book Club
A Division of the Red Helmet Training Group
Rancho Cucamonga, CA 91730
www.FirefighterBookClub.com

ISBN: 978-1-959240-09-9 (Paperback)
ISBN: 978-1-959240-07-5 (Hardback)

Library of Congress Cataloging-in-Publication Data
Library of Congress Control Number

Author – Dennis Reilly
Foreword – Frank Leeb
Cover Photo courtesy of the Cherry Hill Fire Department

Managing Editor – Jesse Quinalty
Copy Editor - Judith Glick-Smith

ENDORSEMENTS

With 50+ years in the fire service in multiple fire departments across the US when Chief Dennis Reilly speaks . . .we should be listening. When Chief Reilly writes, we should be reading. I am excited for this book to be released!

Clark Lamping
Captain, Clark County (NV) Fire Department

As a training chief, I am constantly reminded that the effectiveness of our crews on the fireground is built long before the call; through expectations, preparation, and how we treat one another in the firehouse. *Team + Work = Solution* reinforces those truths in a practical, experience-driven way. Dennis Reilly speaks directly to the importance of trust, accountability, and intentional culture, all of which are imperative to developing capable firefighters and strong officers. This book is a solid reminder that teamwork is not accidental, it is trained, reinforced, and intentionally led every day.

DJ Stone
Training Chief
South Walton Fire Protection District

Chief Reilly takes leadership lessons learned from the military, the fire service, and academia and translates them into easy to digest lessons for aspiring, new, and seasoned fire service leaders alike. A great resource for anyone looking to improve their leadership and team-building!

Rob Backer
Battalion Chief / Owner
Thornton, Colorado

I've known Chief Dennis Reilly for quite a few years and have been fortunate to see firsthand his leadership style and the impact he's had on the fire service. The points that he makes in this book are spot on. He understands the difference between being a leader and simply being a manager.

Chief Dennis Reilly gets it.

Battalion Chief Chad Daily
Kansas City Fire Department
Owner O'Byrne Fireground Training

Chief Dennis Reilly covers the gamete when it comes to building high performing teams. He does not overstate or harp on subjects. The Chief makes a point, gives an example, and continues on. His message is clear and concise; he doesn't need 500 pages to say what he can in 250.

Walt Lewis
Deputy Fire Chief
Orlando International Airport Fire Rescue

Fifty plus years of frontline work in the fire service shape these pages: stories of teams pushed to excellence, cultures built around fire-centric purpose, and the enduring power of performance under pressure. Fire Chief Dennis Reilly invites readers on a journey toward leadership that transforms fire service practice.

Shannon Stone
Fire Chief
Midway Fire District

I first met Chief Reilly in of all places Iraq. We found ourselves serving as special operations medics and operators on the same protective detail based out of Bagdad. Dennis and I, as well as all of our teammates, depended on each other to be technically competent, always oriented, and willing to do whatever it took to benefit the team and get all of us home alive.

Chief Reilly has taken an incredible, deep dive into teams, tactics, strategy, leadership, mentoring and even everyday little things that make your operations go smooth, at both a personal and team/organizational level. If you want every single trick of trade that can help your team, your officers and your organization succeed then you are in the right place, because this book does just that.

Chase N Sargent MPA-C, SOM, NRP
Division Chief/Paramedic Commanding Officer
Special Operations Division (Ret)
Virginia Beach Fire and Rescue Services

Safety is a built by-product of competence. Chief Reilly provides proven ways to bring competence to your team. The more competent you and your crew are the more inherently safe you and your crew will be, Chief Reilly can help achieve this goal and, in the process, help your team to be great.

Battalion Chief Micah Horton
Carson City Fire Department
Co - Owner Hortons & Hunt

Chief Reilly puts a focus on organizational respect through competency. This respect trumps rank. The Chief shows ways one can EARN both.

Captain Jesse Horton
Carson City Fire Department
Co - Owner Hortons & Hunt

As we advance through the ranks and our responsibilities within the organization change, it's easy to forget where we started. Team + Work = Success discusses how important it is for leaders to remain humble enough to recall their days of cleaning toilets and doing the grunt work after a fire. Chief Reilly shows that when we take the time to get to know our new and younger members, when we are willing to work alongside them, we will be reminded of where we came from.

Todd Edwards
Battalion Chief (Ret.) Atlanta Fire
Owner Fire Life Training

DEDICATION

To my wife Ann, without your love and support I would not have been able to accomplish a fraction of the success we have enjoyed.

To my children, Patrick & Kelley, my desire to be a good example made me work as hard as I have. Without your presence in my life the outcome might have been very different.

To the men and women of the American Fire Service, I hope this book helps you in executing the critical mission of protecting life and property. If you find any value here the many decades of all the hard work shall have been worth the cost.

ACKNOWLEDGEMENTS

As you read this book you will see that I mention many great firefighters by name. For everyone I mention there are many others who have helped and influenced me. I need to acknowledge the support, wisdom, and kindness the named and unnamed professionals have shown to me. Without their willingness to share, to include me in their circle, this book simply would not have happened.

I have been a member of multiple fire departments in my career. Every step along the journey has helped me develop into the professional that I have become. Thank you for all that you have given me.

It is hard to single people out, almost like picking your favorite child. As hard as this it, at the same time it is pretty easy for me. Thank you, Montrell Haldeman, Bob Giorgio, and Jeremey Criner. IYKYK.

Chief Dennis Reilly and Chief Frank Leeb

FOREWORD

Leadership Matters, and It Always Will

By Chief Frank Leeb

In the pages of this book, Chief Reilly draws on nearly five decades of experience, sharing his thoughts, observations, and the wisdom he has gained along the way to deliver a powerful guide to building successful teams. One of the most impactful aspects of this work is how he weaves personal stories into team-building lessons, bringing each concept to life with clarity and authenticity. His real-world experiences are woven throughout the book as compelling examples that reinforce the principles and strategies he shares. Importantly, he also incorporates the stories and insights of other respected members of the fire service, not simply relying on his own experiences, making this book a true collective of frontline leadership wisdom.

Chief Reilly has a rare ability to absorb what he learns from both within and outside the organizations he's served and distill that knowledge into practical, actionable guidance. I'm honored not only to call Chief Reilly a friend but also to have been entrusted with reading and commenting on this manuscript before publication—and now, to write this foreword.

The principles of strong team building are often simple in theory but challenging to put into practice. The principles and strategies outlined in this book provide a clear, structured path forward. Whether you're building your first team or have had the opportunity to build several, this book offers valuable insight and grounded wisdom.

From culture and trust to team dynamics, training, and even roll calls, Chief Reilly shares what has worked—and what hasn't—throughout his distinguished career in the fire service. From new firefighter to chief of the department, he has lived every level of leadership and brings a depth of experience few can match. He addresses key elements, including setting expectations, fostering responsibility, building trust, ensuring accountability, and establishing metrics to measure team performance.

Strong team culture and high-performing teams don't happen by accident; they require intentional leadership. In that sense, this book is as much about leadership as it is about team building. It's a timely reminder that leadership matters—and it always will.

This book isn't just a reflection on building high-performing teams; it's a blueprint for developing the kind of leadership that sustains them. Leaders like Chief Reilly.

TABLE OF CONTENTS

Introduction....1
Purpose and Focus....7
Picking The Players....17
Culture....23
Trust....35
The Firehouse....45
Roll Call....59
Team Dynamics....73
Training....83
Mindset....99
High Performing Teams....115
The Finer Points....129
Relationships....141
Bullets for the Bosses....151
Epilogue....165
About the Author....169

INTRODUCTION

There are few endeavors that are more team centric and have a higher consequence for failure than the fire service. We live in a team environment and that environment has a direct impact on the service we deliver. If you have a high functioning firehouse, then you will have a solid team and will do good work on the fireground. We must acknowledge that the converse of this statement is also true. If you work at a dysfunctional firehouse, then your chances for success on the fireground are totally dependent on luck.

To an extent, some leaders probably just think team building is something that will naturally happen but building a high performing team is not that easy. Hard work is required to turn a group of individuals wearing the same tee shirt into a high performing team. To assume this will just happen on its own is nothing short of delegation of one's duty. Team building is a critical skill for firefighters and fire officers, but unfortunately it is a skill that often gets overlooked on the training schedule.

I have seen firsthand what happens when we fail to develop the skills and qualities needed to build a high performing team and this is why I have written this book.

In the pages that will follow I offer time tested and results proven tools you can use to build your team. Some of the suggestions might not work for you based on your position, the members or your team or your organizational culture. There is no secret recipe for building a high performing team. You can have all the right ingredients but if you don't apply them correctly you might not get what you set out to achieve. You must do the work required and that is what I explain in each of the chapters. You will find concepts, but you will also find examples that show how you can use the concepts.

So, before we go too far let's define what we mean when we say a high-performing team. Just because you all wear the same tee shirt and ride on the same rig doesn't mean you have a high-performing team. High-performing teams live around shared expectations and accountability. They are focused on the future and what they can do to be a little bit better than they were today. These teams know that people depend on them to be at their best in difficult and dangerous situations. They do not back down at the critical hour, they find a way to deliver no matter what.

As much as high-performing teams focus on their outcomes, they realize that the members of their teams are the critical link between expectations and performance. These teams value their members and do the work necessary to make sure everyone understands their role and can do their job. The human element is what really gets the job done and this fact is not lost in high-performing teams.

It's easy to say, "I am just a firefighter, this isn't my job." Chase Sargent is a retired Division Chief from the Virginia Beach Fire Department and a good friend of mine. Chase taught me an important lesson about saying "it's not my job." He says that the person who says this knows there is a problem and can define the problem and offer a solution. They also know when things go sideways, they will not be the one held accountable for the outcome. It's your firehouse, so yes, it's your problem. I say to everyone who rides a fire engine, you have a role in building your team.

I do not claim to have all the answers when it comes to building high-performing teams, and I would caution listening to anyone who makes such a grandiose claim. Along with my successes in team building, I have had my share of failures. What I will share with you in the following pages are my thoughts and observations on what worked for me. These lessons have been compiled over the span of close to five decades, in ranks from the most junior member of an organization all the way up to fire chief. Not everything is going to fit every situation. I encourage you to use this boom like a menu. Take what you think will work and leave behind what you think will not.

At the end of each chapter, I will leave you with a few nuggets (a term I borrowed from my good friend Chief Shannon Stone) that summarize the key points of the chapter. If you focus on these points, then you will get the key elements of each chapter. The bullets are the fundamental steps to doing the work of building a high performing team.

If you have come looking for the silver bullet to solve all your team's problems, I hate to tell you that you have come to the wrong place. Building a high-performing team takes a lot of work. You must be willing to play the long game. You must work hard every day to make sure the team is where it needs to be, and it stays there. The work never stops, but the need to perform difficult tasks in life threatening situations is always there. The work is hard, but this book will offer many suggestions that you can use to make the task doable. You will find information on building a positive culture, setting expectations, maintaining accountability, conducting effective training, and several other topics that will help you build a high-performing team. If this is what you have been looking for, welcome, you have come to the right place.

The end state of your work will be success, but what does success look like? It is very hard to build the team and do the work if you do not have a clear vision of what the end state will be. I define success as a multifaceted item. Success means that you will be able to deliver what your community expects. Your team will deliver a high-quality service to those who call 9-1-1. Maybe the run is just helping Mrs. Smith get back into her recliner or maybe it is a three-story apartment building with children tapped on the third floor. The nature of the incident doesn't really matter.

Mrs. Smith has the same expectations as the mother of the children at the apartment building. What you do at the small incidents is exactly what you will do at the life-threatening incidents. If you have a sub-performing team on the "routine" calls your people are not going to jump into a phone booth and come out with an S on their chest just because the dispatch notes say people trapped.

Success is also about building an environment that excites people. If you hate your firehouse, you will not be very successful in doing your job. Building a high-performing team is as much about environment as it is about performance. You will never be able to attract or retain high-performing team members if you have a lousy firehouse environment. The time you spend before the bells hit will determine everything that happens after the dispatch. I will offer many suggestions that you can use to be successful in your efforts to build a positive firehouse environment.

The last thing I will mention about success is the personal satisfaction you will get from being successful in the firehouse and on the emergency scene. I don't think anyone who comes into the fire service is all right with being less than successful. Unfortunately, some people land in an environment that is not conducive to producing good results and attracting those motivated people who can deliver at the critical events & times. The greatest joy I think a leader can have is to see their people succeed. When people are successful, they produce good results and are more likely to help and mentor those around them. For our service to succeed we must be concerned about what the service will look like after we leave.

If you don't focus on the long term, you are probably in it for yourself. People who concentrate on the I and not we, do not contribute to a high-performing team. I offer my suggestions to help you be successful, deliver the quality service your community expects, and build a team that will continue to pursue excellence after your tenure is over.

Good luck as you go about the critical work of building a high-performing team. Don't worry about your rank or lack of rank because anyone in any position can step up and be a leader. Hopefully, you will find suggestions contained in these pages that will lead you to success, both as individual and as member of a high-performing team.

PURPOSE AND FOCUS

Anyone who joins a fire department should have a clear understanding of the purpose and focus of their chosen endeavor. The truth is this is not always the case. Many people come to the fire service with high hopes of serving their community. Some people join because they are looking for a hobby, something to do, and do not understand the demanding nature of emergency services delivery.

Clyde Gordon, a long-serving District Chief at the Houston Fire Department, tells the story about when he first joined the fire service. Clyde was simply looking to get a discount at the local pizza joint which was extended to the local volunteer firefighters. Being a big fan of pizza like most people, Clyde started his fire service journey as merely a way to save some money. Many decades later I must say Chief Gordon has grown into one of the finest chief officers in the American fire service, but his story underscores my point; purpose and focus can mean different things to different people.

As we start our conversations about team building, it is appropriate to use a military term. Let's define the end state. High-performing teams must have a clear vision of their purpose, what I call the end state. This end state must be tangible, clearly defined, and readily apparent when you see it. The end state must be known to everyone, and the leader should never assume everyone knows what the end state will look like. Just making a blanket statement like "we are going to be a great engine/truck/squad company etc." does little to guarantee an effective end state.

The end state for effective fireground operations must be clearly defined by expectations and measured by realisticc and appropriate meterics.

There are two tools that will help a team meet their desired end state, expectations, and metrics. Let's look at expectations first and then dive into metrics.

There is an old saying that goes along the lines that you will never know if you have arrived if you don't know where you are going. Expectations not only define the end state, but they also provide tools one can use to get to the end state.

Many officers write expectations memos that tend to be very specific and task focused. I am not all that convinced this is the best route to take. I think it is very presumptuous to judge them as wrong. Based on culture and audience, it might be necessary to make your expectations very detailed. In other settings, this might not be the case. If you are going to be the leader of a team, then you must figure out what is the best fit for taking your team to the desired end state.

Company officers carry the responsibility as well as the accountability for the performance of their team. You put yourself and your team in a very bad position if you have not clearly identified the desired end state in writing to your assigned members. Giving people a written expectations memo does many positive things. First and foremost, it makes the leader spend some time thinking about what the end state should really be. As I have been promoted through the ranks, I have gained some real clarity about my purpose and focus by writing expectations memos. Secondly your assigned members now have a clear picture of what is expected of them. If you don't set expectations and define the end state, then people will naturally do what they think is right.

This is all well and good until someone does something the officer does not like. Now human nature kicks in and there is a good chance that the officer gets mad because of the member's behavior. We have now set the stage for a conflict, and things could spiral downward very quickly. When approached, the member has the perfect defense when they say, "I didn't know what you expected of me." We have all seen this, and we all know the problems that can follow.

The third point is that when people know what is expected, they are more likely to have a higher level of comfort in the workplace. If you don't know what is expected, then you will spend a lot of time looking over your shoulder. This does not produce high-performing, aggressive firefighters who can dominate a high-threat / high-risk event.

As you draft your expectations memo remember you are part of the big picture. I would advise that you review your expectations memo with your boss. The simple question is, can we die on this hill? Let me give you an example. I know of officers who will say in their expectations memo that "you are expected to be here an hour before shift starts." As your boss I would ask "are you going to pay them the extra hour of overtime? I am all about getting in early, but from the legal standpoint you can't order someone to do that. Now can you build the culture within your team that makes the members want to be there early? You bet, and that is what we will explore in this book. Just use caution as you draft your expectations so that when that one person shows up, you can defend everything in your document.

Just because you aren't the officer does not mean you cannot be part of setting expectations to meet the end state. It is a very powerful message when the senior member meets a newly assigned firefighter as they walk into the firehouse on their first tour. A friendly welcome can ease the sense of uncertainty that is natural when someone comes into a new work group. High-performing teams value relationships between their members and starting off with a cheerful welcome is not a bad way to begin to build relationships.

When the senior member is in tune with the company's desired end state, they can start to introduce the subject in an informal way. How would you feel if on your first day in a new firehouse you were met by the senior member who said:

"The boss is going to sit down with you and go over expectations. I just want to let you know I support the boss and I will do anything I can to help you get in sync with how this firehouse operates. We've got a great company here and this could very well be the best assignment you ever have. Welcome to Rescue 13C."

Not only do high-performing teams have a clear vision of their end state, but they also define metrics to gauge their performance. They regularly test their capabilities against these metrics to ensure maximum fireground performance. They are honest with each other and when they come up short on meeting their metrics, they do the work to correct their behaviors. Most importantly, they know that weak teams rest on past performance and high-performing teams have a forward-looking focus.

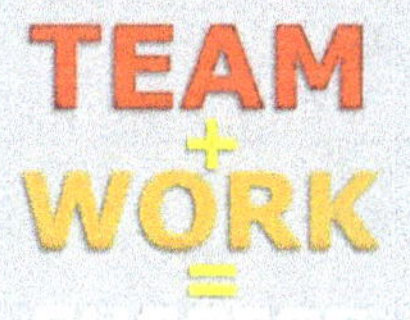

Not only do high-performing teams have a clear vision of their end state, but they also define metrics to gauge their performance.

The metrics that I speak of can be both very specific to a particular location and/or a type of company or general in nature that can apply to any team engaged in firefighting. One of the basic tests I recommend for all engine companies is to set a time standard for the deployment of each of your preconnected hose lines.

The normal staffing complement, the design and layout of the hose bed, and the hose loads and sizes of the company will all impact this standard. It is unwise to make a blanket statement if all these factors are not uniform across a department. I also feel strongly that having a company standard will focus your work on improvement inward. The company should ask themselves how they can get better and not be preoccupied with just being a little faster than their neighboring companies. Truck companies can look at a time standard for deploying any size ground ladder they carry and making it to the roof of a structure, ready to conduct ventilation operations.

Setting metrics that will be truly effective in gauging a team's performance to fulfill the department's core purpose is more complicated than just setting a time standard. Too often, we see this standard set and tested at the fire department's drill grounds. Here, a company operates in a wide-open space, advancing their line into a sterile burn building to a specific location. Let's say the company responds to a neighborhood where most houses have basements, and they see a considerable amount of basement fires. If the metric for deploying the handline is tested to the end state being the first floor of a burn building, the metric has little value in determining how this company will operate at a working basement fire. Likewise, if a response local contains two-story houses, the first-floor metric will lack credibility for judging overall company performance.

Use caution in developing your metrics. Firefighters are extremely intelligent, and if your metrics do not accurately represent the fires the companies respond to, the metric will merely become a "check the box" exercise.

Ladder companies must be able to carry, position, and raise ground ladders in difficult situations. Cars, fences, narrow alleys, and overhead wires present many challenges that affect the time it takes to position a ladder. It is rare to see a training center set up with these obstacles and then have companies perform their time evolutions in this environment. If we expect our members to perform in challenging situations, then we must give them the opportunity to train in like conditions.

As beneficial as pre-incident metrics are, consideration should also be given to developing a means to gauge actual fireground performance. One of the most relevant performance measures, and thus supporting the fire department's purpose, is the time between the first unit's arrival and the victim's removal. Chief Brian Brush of the Midwest Fire Department as part of the working group of The Firefighter Rescue Survey Project have provided the fire service with objective, undeniable data about the positive impact on victim survivability these two variables have on each other. As the time between unit arrival and victim removal decreases, victim survivability increases.

For an organization that is charged with saving life, this metric can be very telling when it comes to operational effectiveness.

High-performing teams, by their very nature, will seek to improve their performance as it relates to relevant markers. It is also worth noting that even as time increases, there still is a notable victim survivability factor. At the twelve-minute mark, there is still a fifty percent chance for survival. High performing teams will have a “stay in the fight” mentality and this data point suggest the value of this mindset.

Saving life is most definitely the top priority of the fire service, but we should not lose sight of the fact that property has value to those who are experiencing the fire. Saving a family bible or photos of loved ones who have passed away can make a horrific event a little more tolerable for those who are victims of a fire.

One of the most effective means to do this is to track fire spread from the arrival of the first due company to when the fire is placed under control. There is a big difference between performing a task on the drill ground and performing the same tasks at the scene of a working fire. The leader's goal should be to reduce the time it takes from when the first unit arrives until the incident is placed under control. Unlike the task-specific metrics, this standard can be applied to any incident. A motor vehicle collision with entrapment can be measured the same way as a house fire. The important element here is to understand the concept of what is measured is more likely to be done.

When we clearly define the purpose of our team, the next step is to ensure all members focus on that purpose. Members of the fire service come to the firehouse with all the elements of their lives. It is totally unreasonable to expect them to shut off all the influences of their lives simply by pulling into the firehouse parking lot. The leaders of the team, be they the formal or the informal leaders, need to accept the responsibility of getting their assigned members to focus on the mission and maintain that focus throughout the tour of duty. This text will offer many practical steps that can be taken to do this, but the most important step is to understand the importance of gaining focus and maintaining that focus as the team moves through their day.

Chapter Nuggets

- Don't assume everyone in your firehouse has a clear understanding of the purpose and focus of your command.
- Metrics can help you determine if your command is meeting its mission.
- Metrics must be relevant to the mission, the company, and the response local where you operate.
- The good teams don't look to be better than other teams, they look to be the best they can possibly be with what they have.

PICKING THE PLAYERS

A team's strength lies in its members and their ability to coalesce into an effective fighting force. It is totally unrealistic to think that everyone who wears the uniform of your department will be a meat-eating go-getter. That would be nice, but it just doesn't happen. Nick Sirianni, the coach of the Philadelphia Eagles says, "Great teams are made up of great teammates." As you build your team, one of your driving forces should be to attract those who can walk the walk and make your firehouse less appealing for those who don't share the passion and dedication for the job.

Different departments have different means of deciding who goes where. Every system has its strengths and weaknesses. One variation is a system where assignments are decided on a bid process that is driven by seniority. It is easy to find faults with seniority-based systems. Here is where you find candidates for promotion using the dreaded "well, I've been here the longest, so it's my turn to get promoted" answer when asked what makes them qualified to be promoted.

The absolute upside to the seniority-based system is that the "corner mutts," as retired Deputy Chief Viscuso of the Kearny, NJ Fire Department refers to them, will not bid into a hard-driving team environment. These people are looking for an easy button career. If your firehouse is known as a hardworking, all-in operation, it is highly unlikely to see the mutts beating a path to the door of your firehouse.

In many departments, headquarters determines fire station assignments and transfers people as they see fit. This can cause a lot of frustration for the company officers and others assigned to a particular firehouse, but there are several things one needs to consider in this type of system. You are viewing the world through a narrow sight glass.

Headquarters must view many pros and cons when making assignments, and you might not be aware of all these considerations. The needs of the community trump what you may or may not want and who you want in your firehouse. Understand that you are just one piece in the larger puzzle. I have often told officers, "You've got to play the hand you are dealt." Through the remainder of this book, I will offer suggestions and techniques to help alleviate some of the problem situations you might find yourself in when it comes to getting new people assigned to your command. Remember your true character as a professional will be on full display when transfers are announced. Act like a spoiled kid, and that impression will stay with your boss for a long time.

One of the best ways to insulate yourself from problems at transfer time is to work hard every day. I do not know of many fire chiefs who would deliberately go about breaking up an outstanding company just because they are an outstanding company. Fire Chiefs are very aware that the ultimate responsibility for a community's fire protection rests with them (or at least one would hope the fire chief realizes this). If you have a solid firehouse and a high-performing team, your department's administration is going to be aware of this. The simple question is, why would the fire chief move people around that would dilute a solid fireground asset? If you want to keep your team intact, work hard every day to be a great fireground company.

The downside to having a strong team, and what is somewhat contradictory to the point I just made, is there is a chance you might be the place that the less optimal members are assigned. Sometimes, exposing the marginal performers to high-performing teams will help them reassess their vision of our profession. It's no fun having to deal with these folks, but there are several points to consider. Primarily, this action says that the chief has a lot of confidence in what is happening with your team. Take that as a huge compliment and go about seeing how you can help the department and yes, the person who is coming to your command as the department's science project. Sometimes a potentially great firefighter simply ends up at the wrong firehouse.

This "problem employee," as some would label them, could very well be a great firefighter, a solid employee, and an asset to the community. They just ended up in a work group where they couldn't rise to their potential. Have your expectations clearly defined in writing for these folks? Put them on a short leash but give them a clean slate to show what they can truly offer to your team.

The work you do inside your firehouse spreads outside the walls of your physical building. As you work to develop a high-performing team, other members of your department are sure to notice. No firehouse exists in a vacuum. Remember that if you have a high-quality team, you have high-quality teammates. At some point, the rock stars on your team will move on to other assignments.

These go-getters are the very type of people who get promoted. Subject matter experts might get drafted to the training division to help shape organizational culture. As depressing as this might sound to you, take heart that the reputation you are building will attract other like-minded firefighters. It is totally unrealistic to expect to go through your career without some element of change. The work you are doing building a high performing team is very likely to keep the momentum going as you experience turnover among your members.

We all tend to focus on our workspace and the impact that assignments, transfers, and promotions will have on us. Human nature is what it is, and it would be foolish to dismiss this simple fact. What I will say is the hard work you do in building your team will have a ripple effect throughout your department. We want hard-charging, go-getters at our firehouse. The reality is that at some point these type A meat eaters are very likely to move on. The concern really isn't about so and so moving on, it is about who is going to replace that person when they leave.

As you build your team, pursue excellence, and become the go-to company in the fire department, other companies will notice what you are doing. There are countless examples of how the evolution of one company has had positive impacts on other companies within the fire department. As you dial up your game others will not want to be left behind. Not everyone is going to buy into this, but I guarantee you some will. What you are doing today is building a culture where the bench gets deep. When that stellar firefighter gets promoted there will be another meat eater out there just waiting to have the opportunity to transfer into your firehouse.

Hard work always pays off in the end.

Chapter Nuggets

- No matter how you feel about it, change will eventually come to your firehouse.
- If you build a high performing team, the mutts will do what they can to avoid being assigned to your firehouse.
- Building a strong team can create a "feeder system" within your organization and enhance the quality of personnel assigned to your command.

CULTURE

By no means do I consider myself a subject matter expert on culture, but I am smart enough to listen to those who are. From numerous conversations, I have developed a down-and-dirty street-level understanding of culture and how it impacts the team. If you want to build a high-performing team, then you must have some understanding of culture and do the hard work necessary to build a culture that supports your team.

There are many facets of culture, but to have an intelligent conversation, we must first define what culture really means. You can read numerous textbooks on the subject, and you will find many different definitions of culture. At the end of your research, you might not be any more certain than when you started. What this tells me is that we should use our research as a baseline but develop our own working definition for what culture means to our team. For me culture is the base that we use to make critical decisions, guide our actions, and regulate our behavior when no one is looking.

Maybe the people at Harvard University would take exception to this definition but they are not living in a firehouse, making runs, and living in the world in which we live. I want my definition to stay within the bounds of accepted wisdom but be stated in a way that the blue collar, lunch box firefighter who shows up at my firehouse can understand. I think this definition fits the mold. Good people will respect hard work. If you take a little time defining what culture means to your team, professionals will notice your investment. Firefighters are very smart and if you just copy and paste someone else's work it will not carry the weight of an original thought that you have crafted.

Remember we are trying to recruit quality members to our team. When we invest time and effort it is much more likely that good people will migrate to our firehouse and be willing to do the hard work we need them to do. The renewed organizational culture expert Peter Drucker has said "Culture eats strategy for breakfast" so take some time and put some effort into this critical aspect of team building.

Of all the elements that build a culture, values are the cornerstone. Values are the underlying force that shapes the culture and as such are very important. Almost all fire departments have some type of organizational values. As a fire chief, I wrote such value statements for my organization and felt this to be a critical part of building the organization's culture. As important as I see this process, I also must be a realist. Many firefighters will see the core values statement as just something else coming out of Headquarters.

There is a real need to make a supporting connection between the organization's core values and the values at the company level. People relate to what is right in front of them. Defining company values (fig. 3–1) is the link between what the fire chief envisions and what happens in the fire house.

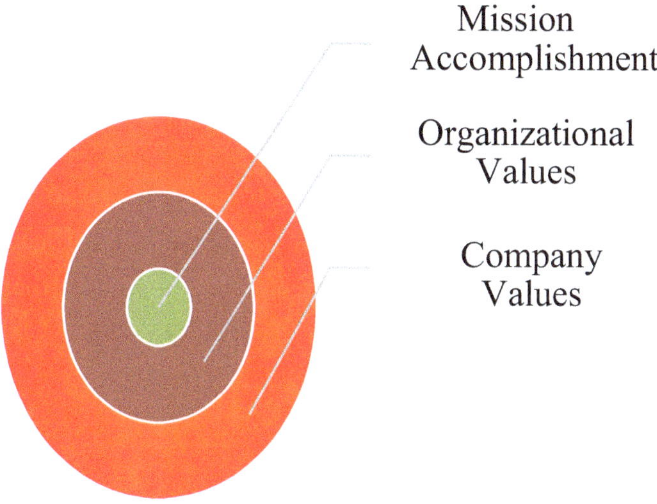

Figure 3–1: Defining company values

Defining values at the company level gives your members a tool that will help them align with the overall organizational values and support mission accomplishment. Allow me to connect the dots between the organization's values and the intermediate values in the firehouse. What we want to do is draw a strong connection between the two that our members can relate to.

Let's say our organizational core values are:

- Courage
- Commitment
- Honor

(For all the Marines out there, yes, this Army guy borrowed these from the Corps. Semper Fi)

These are solid values that will allow us to deliver the service our community expects, but they can be somewhat vague and kind of lofty. How many people are going to say that they are cowards, lazy, or dishonest? In all my roles as a subordinate officer, be it a company officer or battalion chief, I tell my members that in this command we would value:

- Trust
- Tactical excellence
- Team above self
- Hard work

These four values align with the organizational values, but they tend to be a little more visible at the everyday team level. Work with a person for a few shifts and you will know right off if they can be trusted. Everyone on this team will see firsthand how each other performs at an incident thus giving everyone a means to judge each other's tactical excellence.

It doesn't take long to figure out if a newly assigned member is a team player and if the recliner they sit in is hot enough to bake cookies you know that they don't embrace hard work.

Values are important but there are other elements that make up the culture in a command. Fig. 3–2 is a graphic depiction of what I think are the critical elements of culture within an operational unit. As I have already stated, this is not the only model, it is the one I have used with a lot of success in the past.

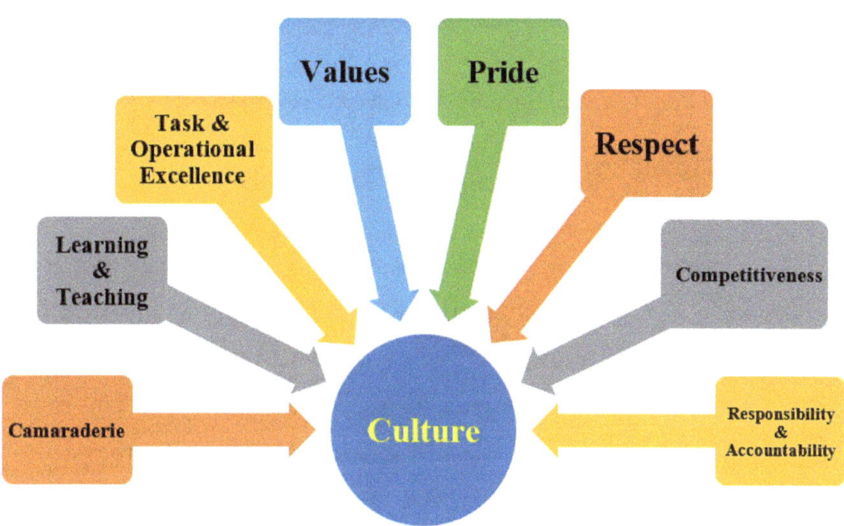

Fig. 3–2: Culture defined.

On the following pages I will break down my definitions for each of the items in this chart.

Camaraderie

We all have a responsibility to make the workplace somewhere that we do not dread, but that we enjoy. We spend too much time at the firehouse to accept anything less. Our strength on the fireground is built in the firehouse, and that requires work. There will always be personalities and sometimes conflicts. These cannot be allowed to fester over time. Our profession is a brother/sister hood. We should embrace this. We should strive to build relationships that support the brother/sisterhood. If you are miserable in your job, then maybe you need to look inside for the cause. If you have a hard time getting along with a lot of folks, it is highly unlikely you are right and everyone else is wrong.

Learning and Teaching

Nobody knows everything. Our working environment is constantly evolving. Every member of this organization is expected to be a subject matter expert. You must keep an open mind, and you must stay abreast of the current best business practices. You must also be willing to listen to a good idea, even if it comes from someone less senior or maybe someone you do not like. The knowledge we have does not belong to us. We are stewards of this knowledge, and we will pass this along to those who follow in our footsteps. Part of our fundamental professional responsibility is to prepare our replacement. Share all that you know. It will only make us better. Those who use knowledge as power have no place in our culture.

Task and Operational Excellence

Everyone must master their basic skill set. As you progress in your career, that set expands, but you are still expected to retain what you already know. A Chief Officer might not be expected to pull a hose line or throw a ladder in the normal performance of their duties, but as the Marine Corps says, "Every Marine is a Rifleman."

Operational brilliance means that you can take those elements in your skill set and apply them in a dynamic /high-risk environment. If you are a firefighter, you should be able to perform engine or truck tasks without flaws. If you are a company officer, you should be able to deploy and lead your company to provide the possible outcome for those who call for help. If you are a Chief Officer, you should be able to command a difficult event by making good decisions with incomplete data, in compressed time frames, while managing the risk to which your people are exposed.

Values

Values are our underlying principles. They are what drive our decisions and what we will not compromise. Values determine how you will act when no one is watching or when you must make a critical decision that has ramifications that go past the end of your nose. If we call ourselves an organization that exists to provide excellent service, then that must be our driving force. Shared values bind us together, and they are what make us a cohesive team. Everything else flows from our values, and we must spend time each day talking about and reinforcing the concept of values. If we fail to do this, then all else will be for nothing.

Pride

Pride is a direct reflection of your company, your battalion, and your organization. We do not settle; we do not accept good enough. If we commit to a task, then we commit to the effort to get it done right the first time. Our stations, our apparatus and equipment, our uniforms and appearance are all pieces of the whole, and they all matter.

What we will not do is let pride get in the way of the other aspects of our culture. We will be open to honest, objective criticism. We will take this without taking it personally. Our pride does not equate with superiority.

Respect

Everyone, regardless of rank or seniority, has a voice and a right to be heard. If you are honest and caring, trying to help the organization, and focused on the mission, we will listen to what you have to say. Not everyone's suggestions will be adopted, but your opinions will not be dismissed just because of who you are.

Everyone has a right to a safe and stable workplace. Respect is what makes that happen. As much as respect is a fundamental part of culture, you must do your part. If you are the malcontent, if you do not show respect to others, if you turn your back on all that is included in this document, you will find it hard to fit in with those who respect the concept of culture.

Competitiveness

We will use competition as a tool for improvement. Our biggest competitor is ourselves. Are we doing everything we can do to be the best firefighters we can? Are we putting in the effort at the company level to make the most of the talent we have on our rig? It's always nice to beat the other man or woman, but most champions focus on themselves, not others. Competition should always be healthy, never mean-spirited, or malicious. If you come out on top, offer suggestions to the second-place company to help them improve. If you are the second-place company, ask the winner how they did it and what you can improve. Our most important show time is when the bells hit, and we must be able to pull together as a cohesive fighting team to achieve success on the fire ground.

Responsibility and Accountability:

Everybody needs to know their job and do their job. This is the simple definition of responsibility. Our mission is of such a critical nature we do not have time to tell a member to do what they should already know. Our supervisors are not here to herd cats. They have responsibilities as leaders and cannot afford to babysit professionals.

True accountability is trusting that your people are doing their jobs and that they arc operating in the area that they were assigned to. It has nothing to do with Tags, Velcro, Rings or Magnets.

Jesse Quinalty
Strategies and Tactics for Employee Fires

As much as we believe in responsibility, we acknowledge that our members are humans and mistakes will be made. The expectation is that if something happens less than our expectations, the member in question will be accountable for what happened. We must view these occurrences as learning experiences, not an automatic career ending event. It is never acceptable to hide a mistake, shift responsibility to someone else, or lie about it. One of the quickest ways to remove yourself from an organization is to hide, defer, or lie about something.

Culture is a complex issue that requires a clear vision and a lot of hard work. The effort you expend on building the culture of your team will lead to operational success, increased firefighter safety, and personal and professional satisfaction. Isn't that why we are here? Excellent organizations spend more time working on culture than anything else. Nothing is a given and the mere desire to have something does not guarantee results. Hard work and consistency are the keys. Let's roll up our sleeves and get after it.

Chapter Nuggets

- High-performing teams have a strong culture.
- Good team culture requires hard work by the leader to make the culture happen.
- Values are the underlying fallback drivers of behaviors.
- You must define the elements you want to make up your culture and then clearly explain what each of them means to your team.

TRUST

For a team to function at a high level in a demanding situation, there must be trust between members of the team. At some point, when our backs are up against the wall we will look to our left and our right. Who we see and how we think about them will have a tremendous impact on the outcome. Trust in the firehouse rises above our personal feelings, but we are all human and subject to how we feel about the people with which we work. To build trust we must invest effort over time. Trust is not built overnight, and it is not a by-product of what we say. Trust is the result of the actions we take day in and day out. Trust is a two-way street, from the firefighters to the officer and from the officer to their firefighters.

Let's look at what builds trust in a high performing team.

Engaging at a structure fire can be a very dangerous undertaking. In Maslow's Hierarchy, the first level of human needs is known as safety needs. The people on the team must have faith that their leader is a competent decision maker on the emergency scene. In the simplest terms the team needs to be able to say: "Our officer knows what they are doing, he/she isn't going to get us killed." Officers have a moral obligation to the people they lead to be tactically proficient and maintain calmness in high-stress situations. These attributes are not something that gets issued with a badge and collar brass. It takes hard work on the part of the officer to develop and maintain these skills.

Successful officers/team leaders are students of the craft. They not only understand the tasks and tactics of the fireground, but they also understand the human dynamics of the decision-making process in the environment. This topic has been written about extensively, and I am by no means an expert who can take a deep dive into this. My point here is to acknowledge the importance for officers to be good decision makers and encourage you to include this topic in your professional development.

The second thing officers need to consider is having a genuine concern for your members professionally. There are very few times I will use the word *never* but now is one of the rare occasions. Never tell your people "I don't care" about anything they bring to your attention. I have seen officers use this term on several occasions and every time it has had a very negative impact on the individual member and the team as a group. For the individual member it demonstrates the leader is not willing to listen to new ideas. The status quo is perfectly acceptable in that command and there is little anyone can do to influence the leader.

Strong teams are always looking for a way to get better and when you say I don't care to a member who is trying to help the team improve, you are cementing your current position as the way your team will always do business. Not only does this comment stifle the individual member, but it can also be quite embarrassing for a member when that is said in front of their peers. There is nothing wrong with saying "I don't agree," "I'm not sure that will work here," "We are not ready to move in that direction," or a whole host of other things; just don't say "I don't care."

Caring for your members professionally is important but remember they are also people. I don't think a leader should strive to be best friends with everyone on their team, but if you are going to be an effective leader there is some amount of concern you should show your members on a personal level.

Saying happy birthday, asking about a child's baseball game, or asking how a spouse is doing after a bout with the flu shows that you care. Caring is one of the building blocks of positive relationships which in turn strengthens the team. These little things can make the workplace somewhere people don't mind spending their time. We ask our team members to sacrifice a lot in the performance of their duties, and showing some concern on the personal level does not come with a downside.

One major responsibility for an officer is to develop the members under their command and allowing them to make decisions is a great way to do this.

I remember a gnarly working fire where all our resources were committed, and we were still getting it handed to us. Our first arriving mutual aid engine arrived, and instead of seeing hard-charging firefighters dismounting the rig and hustling to help us, I watched the company officer stroll down the street like he was on the Saturday trip to the grocery store.

He could tell by the look on my face I was not pleased. His feeble attempt at damage control was "My people don't do anything until I size up the scene and give them direction." If you manage your team this way do not expect your members to take the initiative. There are times when the fight will be won by someone in the right place at the right time using their initiative to shape the outcome of an incident. If you don't empower your people to make decisions, you will lose the force multiplier effect of having multiple decisions operating on your team.

When I speak about this in one of my seminar presentations, I often field the question about what happens if a subordinate makes the wrong decision. Hopefully, you are not working in a zero deficient environment because mistakes will always happen. I ask the people who raise this point if they have never made a mistake, and to my best recollection, no one has ever claimed a perfect record. Well, the world didn't come to an end, and they were not beheaded by their boss. If we develop our members correctly the ramifications of mistakes will almost always be fixable. These so-called gaffes ended up being just one more learning opportunity.

My last point for officers, and one that applies to firefighters building trust with their officers, is to have an adequate level of tactical fitness. This can be a very subjective term and one that can produce some very spirited conversations. Firefighting can be a hazardous endeavor that can put firefighters and officers in life-threatening situations. Should an event go sideways those operating in the hazard zone must have trust that those they work with will be able to handle the situation and get the affected member out of harm's way. If you can't trust the people you ride the rig with to do this, the ability to build trust at the team level will be severely compromised.

This topic can be the subject of a book all by itself, and the intent of this work is not to dive too deeply into tactical fitness. My experience tells me that if you commit daily effort to working on your fitness, in a tough challenging way people will see your effort and give you the credit that your hard work has earned.

As I have said, trust is a two-way street. Officers must do the work to earn the trust of their members, but there is a lot of work the members must do in return to earn the trust of their officers. To start with, firefighters must know how to do their job. Professionals are expected to be able to execute the fundamental elements of their position and if one wants to be accepted by their team, they must know their job. There are way too many things going on at a fire for a company officer to stop and coach a firefighter through a task that should be part of their skill set.

Knowing your job also means being honest about knowing what you don't know. It is an unreal expectation to think someone knows everything. High-performing teams understand this and judge people in part on how they handle the gap between what they know and what they should know. Assuming a member has a decent grasp on their fundamental skill, most officers and their fellow teammates will welcome someone saying, "Hey, guys, I am a little weak with the one-person throw of a 24 ft. ladder, can someone help me tighten up my game"?

Tactical proficiency is a step up from knowing your job and must be the standard for high-performing teams. Knowing how to throw a 24 ft. extension ladder behind the firehouse, at 1400 hours on a sunny day in your station uniform is one thing. Tactical proficiency is the ability to perform basic job functions on the fireground.

Let's take the 24 ft. ladder example and change a few of the details. Instead of it being 1400 hours, it is 0300 hours, and you are on the twelfth run of the day. It's 34 degrees out with the wind blowing and steady rain. Your gear is still wet from a kitchen fire your company was first due to this afternoon, and there are reports of children trapped in the room where you are throwing the ladder. Being able to execute at the exact level, or maybe even a little bit higher than you did behind the firehouse, is tactical proficiency. Without tactical proficiency, you will be hard pressed to have your officer, or your company, place any real trust in you.

Understanding your role on the fireground will help you build trust with your team. Being able to build tempo faster than the fire is growing is a fundamental element of winning the firefight. You should be clear about what your role will be if your company is first due, second due, third due, etc. Having this knowledge will require some pre-incident conversations with the officer and other members of the company.

Strong teams love talking about fires. Taking a deep dive into your individual role lets the people you work with know you are into the job. That's not a bad reputation to have. Knowing your role will also allow the officer to concentrate on the tasks they need to accomplish. Anytime we can make the boss's life easier is an opportunity you should not let pass by.

For your officer to trust you, you must make good decisions. This applies to your off-duty life as well. No one totally separates their firehouse life from their personal life. If you make bad decisions off duty, it is totally unreasonable to expect you to become a great decision maker when you pull into the firehouse parking lot. What you do at home is more than likely what you will do at work. If my life depends on the decisions you make, which is the world where we work, I need to know that you normally make good decisions. Another piece of this puzzle is that for the most part, our lives are open books when we join the fire department. You might think no one knows the details of your life outside the firehouse, but that is not the way things work. If you make terrible decisions off duty, sooner or later those poor decisions will make their way back to the firehouse.

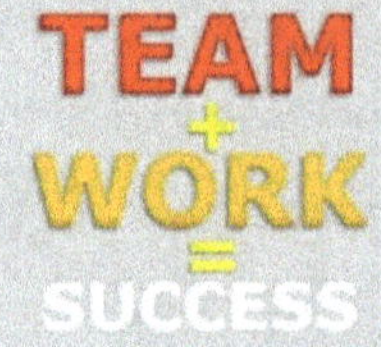

Knowing your job also means being honest about knowing what you don't know.

We can talk about trust in the abstract all day long, but its real value shows up on the fireground. Let me share an example of how trust worked both up and down the chain of command.

When I was a Captain in Cherry Hill, NJ, my ladder company was dispatched as a special call company to a working fire in a large, abandoned hotel complex. The first arriving companies reported what they thought was a working fire in the basement but were confronted with a very confusing building layout and a significant forcible entry challenge. This was one of those fires where seconds truly mattered and if we couldn't reach the seat of the fire quickly the incident could very well spiral out of control.

One of my members had been a security guard at this complex before it went out of business. Tom told me we could access the basement from the Charlie side of the building through a service corridor and felt confident he could lead us to where we needed to go. I had worked with this firefighter for some time and trusted that he knew what he was talking about. I went to the Incident Commander (IC) and asked if he would allow my company to enter the Charlie side of the building and find the seat of the fire. The IC agreed and off we went. With my firefighter leading the way we were able to access the basement, locate the seat of the fire, and open up some doors from the interior to allow the engine companies to reach the seat of the fire. Within a minute or two we were able to gain the upper hand, and the fire went under control.

The successful outcome of what was headed towards a bad day for our department was all about trust. The members of my company trusted me enough to come to me with an out-of-the-box suggestion. I trusted Tom not to put us in a bad situation. I knew what he was saying was risky, but I also felt that we could manage the risk we were taking. My Chief trusted me that I would not put my company at an unnecessary risk. If you are doing the work, building a reputation based on the trust you have earned, you will have an opportunity at some point to show that your team is truly made up of high performers. Even though this complex was not occupied at the time of the fire, it was historically significant to our community. We should not take foolish chances, but our communities trust us to protect their property along with their lives.

Chapter Nuggets:

- High-performing teams are built on trust between the members.
- For Firefighters to trust their officers, the officers must:
    - Make good emergency scene decisions that will not endanger the members.
    - Have a genuine concern for their members professionally and personally.
    - Empower their members to make decisions.
- For officers to trust their members, the members must:
    - Know their jobs.
    - Be tactically proficient.
    - Know their role within the company at first-, second-, and third-due incident.
    - Make good decisions on and off duty.
- All members need to maintain a level of tactical fitness for the others to trust them.

THE FIREHOUSE

A dysfunctional firehouse is the breeding ground for a dysfunctional fireground. Most fire departments spend a limited amount of time engaged in firefighting/emergency response and most of their time back in the firehouse. It is totally unrealistic to think that where you spend most of your time will not affect your operations. There is nothing wrong with using your time in the firehouse getting ready for the next run. In this chapter, I present some of the tools and techniques to build your firehouse into a breeding ground for excellence

Before I dive into the particulars of what I see as important elements in building a healthy firehouse, I must address a growing trend in the fire service. There are textbooks currently in print that say we should no longer use the term firehouse. The book or books say that our firehouses are places of business, that the term firehouse implies ownership and the buildings we refer to do not belong to us, they belong to the community. At the intellectual level it is hard to argue with this logic, but I will offer a counter opinion.

I have always said that we are stewards of what our community provides, and we must never forget that. We should also take to heart that ours is a unique working environment. To be successful in a high-threat / high-stress situation, teamwork is an absolute must. Look at any other high-performing team, and you will find a workplace that is much more than a clean or sterile office environment. Championship team locker rooms, team rooms for military special operation units, and yes, many firehouses take a sense of ownership in their workspace. The walls are adorned with slogans, pictures of past engagements, and mementos of the team's history. To abandon the traditions of our firehouses will in my opinion do little to position us for success on the fireground. Oh well, guess I will never be invited to contribute to future editions of these books, and that is fine by me. Enough of my soapbox speech and back to the work at hand.

The most important step you can take in having a healthy firehouse is to not give up control of your firehouse to someone you have no control over. As strange as this may sound, I see it all the time. How many times have you seen a policy or procedure come out from headquarters that "whips up the troops." You know what comes next from your people "I/we would never do that, why are they wasting time on something as dumb as ….." Most times these policies come out because of something somebody did. As much as we would hope this issue would be handled one-on-one with the offender, maybe that was what the fire chief tried.

In discussing this issue, we must remember that we don't always know all the details of the conversations that have been held about this "infraction." Is it possible that the fire chief tried to handle this as a one-on-one discipline issue, but was stopped by Human Resources because there is no policy in place addressing the "infraction"? If something has happened once there is nothing saying that it could not happen again, the policy that the people in your firehouse are upset about might have been forced into publication by someone other than the fire chief. Whatever the specifics are, just circle back to the quote from the first part of this conversation "I/we would never do something like that." If that's true forget about the policy and go pull some hose.

Let's look at another common piece of firehouse drama. Someone in your firehouse delivered some earth-shattering news they heard at shift change. It is human nature to default to the negative when you hear something. This is a survival instinct that goes back to the days when we were an appetizer for the saber-tooth tigers. Evolution has brought us a long way from those days, but the tendency for about 75 percent of your brain to view things from a negative perspective is still there. This is something I learned a few years ago at a seminar in Kansas City, and to be honest, it really clarifies a lot of stuff for me. Although rumors are grounded in truth, the actual amount of truth along with the negative impacts will most times end up being marginal. When we start to ask some questions, it comes to light that this earth-shattering piece of information comes from a questionable source.

Some people just get stuff wrong. They hear something, and like the childhood game of telephone, when they retell what they heard, it has little semblance to what was originally said. Some people just lie outright. Everyone knows these people are chronic liars, so when you find out that this questionable person is the source of this troubling tidbit, just ask the question "When was the last time (insert name) told the truth"? Could it be possible that this source of information is just trying to stir the pot? There are people who take great joy in watching others twist and turn in the commotion they cause.

Whatever the case, don't play into the drama. When these contentious statements come up, ask a few questions. If the issue is a policy that you would never violate in the first place, why worry about it? If you heard this tidbit from the most unreliable source of information in the firehouse, why are we spending any time on this? If the source is a known liar, what makes you think that they are now, suddenly, turning over a new leaf and have become a trusted source? When you start looking at these things from the thirty-thousand-foot level, they really lose a lot of their significance. When one of these issues comes up, stop it dead in its tracks. If you allow these items to linger, they will take control of your firehouse. Use the counterarguments I mentioned in the first part of this paragraph and then go out and pull some hose or throw ladders. If you keep the energy focused on firefighting tasks, there will not be a lot of energy left for the other stuff.

The firehouse needs to be a place where the assigned members want to be. A big part of building this environment is treating each other well. I am an old school guy, and I do think new people have got to earn their place, but there is a limit to what we should call paying dues. The new members assigned to your firehouse are not indentured servants. They are not there to do the dirty jobs that you think you have outgrown. The new members are not there for your amusement. As my good friend District Chief Mo Davis of the Houston Fire Departments says: "If you got time to flour them, you've got time to train them." We would all be well served to remember that hazing is a degrading behavior forced on members of the team strictly for the amusement of the more senior team members.

A big part of having a firehouse that people want to come to, and don't want to transfer out of, rests in treating each other well. Some of the "old heads" will laugh at this and say, "That wasn't the way it was when I was coming up." I wish I had a dollar every time I heard that. My simple reply is you probably didn't like it when you were coming up so what makes you think it is ok now? In my opinion we ruin a lot of good firefighters with this nonsense.

I have seen this many times to the extent that some of the members on the receiving end were headed to the door, never to come back. Often, when these members find themselves in a positive culture, they flourish.

I know of one example where the "old timers" wrote a firefighter off as being a lost cause and not a good fit. The chief before me decided he would move the person in question. This firefighter is now a captain and a highly respected member of the department. Treating people well should be the standard across the board for all our firehouses.

The little things are what sends a positive message to our people. My good friend John Spera sent me a picture of these folded T-shirts. He got busy working around the firehouse and forgot about his laundry. When he walked into the utility room to finish doing his laundry, he found his stuff dried and folded. I bet I am not the only one who has done this same thing, only to find their clothes in a heap on top of the dryer. I remember one time someone took my wet clothes out of the washing machine and just threw them, soaking wet, on top of the dryer.

Here is another picture from District Chief Clyde Gordon. Chief Gordon works out of Station 8, one of the biggest and busiest in the city. Sunday is the big cleaning day, trucks, bays, and a bunch of other stuff. The Chief could easily just sit in his office and wait for all the work to be done. Instead, Chief Gordon cooks breakfast for the whole station so that once all the work is done everyone can sit down and enjoy a meal together.

Some people will just shrug these simple gestures off, saying things like “I am not here to do someone else’s laundry” or “Hey, because he’s a chief, he doesn't have to do any of the dirty work, that’s the least he can do.”

If you want to take that selfish way of thinking, then I guess you should just stop reading this book right now. Little things go a long way with good people. I can only speak for myself, but if someone folds my laundry, I think, "Hey, I owe them a favor," and I don't mind paying them back. When a ranking officer cooks a meal for me, I say "Wow, he remembers where he came from." Positive energy begets positive energy, and positive energy is a key ingredient for a healthy firehouse.

The firehouse kitchen table has always been one of the true joys of being in the fire service. Many problems have been solved at the table. The kitchen table is where we go for a good laugh, sometimes at our own expense. We gather there to ease the burden of our job, to share the lessons we have learned along our individual journeys, both in the fire service and in life, and build the sense of team that is absolutely necessary for us to be effective on the emergency scene.

With as much as the kitchen table has to offer, we must set some rules for those who wish to have a seat. Your spot must be earned every day, no exception. One of my favorite sayings is, "We only give away two things here, attitude and bubble gum, and we are all out of bubble gum." Your performance last year does not guarantee that your performance tomorrow will be of the same high caliber. You must work hard every day to ensure you can be counted on, and that is why I say you must always earn your seat here. At the table, there is no rank, only respect.

One of the biggest benefits of the kitchen table is the free exchange of information. We have the ability of learning from our past successes and our failures, but this can be hampered if rank is not set aside. I am a big advocate of everyone sitting at the kitchen table without their badges or rank insignia. Everyone knows who the boss is so there is no need to advertise.

However, the absence of the symbols of rank does not signal a free fire zone for the member who just doesn't like the officer. It is quite simple, if you want to be respected for your opinion then you need to respect everyone else, no matter what their standing in the rank structure.

Honesty is an absolute must for everyone at the table. There is always much for each of us to learn, and we should keep in mind a famous quote from Ancient Greece that says, "A man cannot learn something he already thinks he knows." We often have a skewed impression of our own abilities, and to be better, we must be open to the honest feedback that other members of our company can offer. In doing this just remember what was just said in the last paragraph, interactions are done with respect. The goal of the kitchen table is to make everyone better, and this will not happen if we don't offer some common human decency to those with whom we speak. It is also unreasonable to expect people to listen to you if you don't respect others. Temper your words and look to build positive relationships.

All the talk about no rank and respect goes out the window when people let their ego drive their behavior. It is very easy to let rank or experience get the best of us. To this I say, get over yourself! We operate in a team-centric environment where each of us has a role, and each of us depends on one another for our success. I had a lot of power and authority as a Fire Chief, but I always tried to remind myself that the most important members on the emergency scene were our least senior members. When you work in a small department, these folks are the ones who will be making the push with the nozzle or the ones who are doing CPR.

When I was a Fire Chief in Kansas, we held monthly platoon meetings. Sometimes I would have the least senior people stand up and I would remind everyone that these are the people who will be at the pointy end of the spear and our job is to support them. The productive exchange is better accomplished when everyone accepts the importance of each other.

No matter how much we adhere to all these points, human nature is always running in the background. Brand new members may have come from a training environment where they were told not to speak until spoken to. They can be intimidated by the rank and experience that sits with them at the kitchen table. They may also have a fresh set of eyes that sees something we can do a little bit better.

I am not saying a two-month probie should be given carte blanche to change the world, but if they can help our company be a little more efficient at a job, are they not worth listening to what they have to say? For all the probies reading this, refer to item 1. You must earn your seat at the table; no one gets a free pass.

I hear from so many people about how everyone is preoccupied with their phones nowadays, and to be honest, there is a lot of truth in that statement. Just go into any restaurant and look at a table where there is a group of people, and you will probably see them engaged in the 45-degree world, their heads down staring at their phones. Maybe they are doing this because no one says, "hey for the next hour we are going to interact like they did in the old days, by talking with each other."

Strong teams are built on relationships, and relationships are built on interactions. Make a company rule saying that during the meal, unless there is an urgent need for someone, there are no phones or devices. This sounds like an awful big demand but just try it. I have seen this work time and time again. Good conversations and healthy interactions draw people in. Ask the senior member what they think is the most important thing they have learned in their career. Ask the officer what the worst fire they ever went to was, and knowing what they know now, what they would have done differently? Ask the least senior member what the group can help them with in terms of their fireground skills.

All these discussions can start great conversations and build a true sense of team. Before you know it, people will be muting their phones and looking forward to their time at the kitchen table.

If we manage the firehouse the right way, it will add tremendous value to our team. Nobody wants to feel uncomfortable or unwanted in a place where they spend one-third of their lives. Put the effort into making your firehouse a welcoming place, and the effectiveness of your time will be greatly enhanced.

The firehouse kitchen table is one of the best places you will ever be part of, but your seat must be earned every day.

Chapter Nuggets

- A dysfunctional firehouse will surely lead to a dysfunctional fire ground.
- Do not give up control of your firehouse to forces or people you have no influence over.
- People tend to look at the negative in situations, be the adult, and tamp down rumors.
- Set rules for the kitchen table to make it a safe and enjoyable place for your members.

ROLL CALL

Every tour in the firehouse starts with the first hour, and the first hour is an opportunity to set you and your company up for success. Successful teams understand that the smallest advantage can carry the day. Your success on the fireground could very well be determined by how you manage your time in the firehouse, so here are a few suggestions to make that first hour beneficial to mission success.

I must admit that I am a traditionalist, and I see some real value in having a roll call, in the apparatus bay, at the assigned rig. Being a firefighter for most of us is just one facet of our lives. It is totally unrealistic to expect people to leave all the other aspects of their lives in the parking lot when they report for duty. Relationships, children, bills, and family stress can weigh heavily on a person and can impact their ability to perform in critical situations.

Roll call is a great tool to "check in" with the rest of your crew. If you have worked with the same people for any amount of time you can probably tell just by looking at their body language and facial expressions to see if they are ready to go or if there is something going on that might need attention. Roll call is a way for everyone to do a quick "size up" of their co-workers and, let me stress, everyone has a piece of this. The officer holds the formal title and ultimate responsibility for the company's operations, but the senior person may be better positioned to notice and ask questions. Let's make sure that everyone will be ready for the tour.

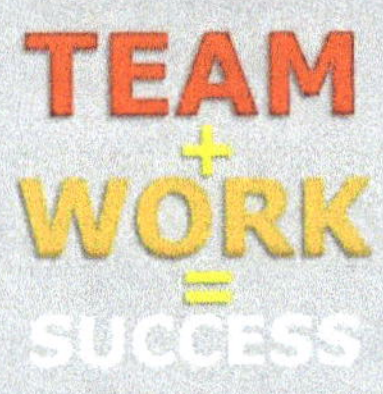

Roll call is a great tool for checking in and sizing up your crew to get everyone focused on the task at hand.
This process is called A.P.E., which stands for reviewing the Apparatus, Personnel, and Equipment.

Having roll call is a great way to not only check in with everyone but also get everyone to focus on the task at hand. This 24 or 48 belongs to the community and everyone needs to focus on that. We have all worked with "Joe the landscaper." Joe is a good guy, but he really isn't into the job. He is here for health insurance and to have a rest day from pushing a lawnmower. As much as we might not like this, it is a reality in many firehouses. This is the time for the officer to send the "this is the time to focus on the fire business" message. Starting the tour off right is taking advantage of the opportunity to take three or four individuals who come to the firehouse with their own ideas and agendas and give them a unified direction in which to move for the tour. I used to like to ask my members a simple question, "Hey (insert name), we are going to make a gnarly fire today with people trapped, are you ready"?

We assume firefighters would be able to say yes to this question but making them verbally commit to their role in front of the other members of the company has the effect of making a contract with the folks they will be living with for the next 24–48 hours. There is some real impact in doing this.

At roll call, reviewing the A.P.E. is critical. The A.P.E. stands for apparatus, personnel, and equipment, and is a concept I learned from the Philadelphia Fire Department. This is simply about putting you and your team ahead of the power curve. Let's look at a few examples. Say your regular chauffeur is on a vacation day, and your backup chauffeur has just passed their certification tests. When you walk into the firehouse after your four-day break, you see your rig is gone, and the reserve is in the "hot spot." Your chauffeur for this tour has never driven the reserve rig. Does this give you some concern? It might be a good idea for the company to load up and go for a short drive around your first due, so the first time your chauffeur drives the rig is not going to a reported house fire with victims trapped.

Maybe your first due ladder apparatus is a tower ladder, but when their rig goes in for maintenance, they get a rear mount stick. There is a big difference in the operational capabilities of these two rigs. I would rather know this before the bells. Are the other officers working today or is someone out on vacation or sick leave? When the normal staffing is not present things can happen other than what you expect. It pays to take a few minutes at shift change to consider what the run down looks like and think about the impact it might have on the fireground.

Equipment is the last part of the A.P.E. process and just like the other two parts, you should know what is and what isn't available and be ready before you need it. Are all the tools and equipment normally assigned to your rig ready for service or is something out for maintenance or maybe was left at Mrs. Smith's house last during the 0300 hours medical run.

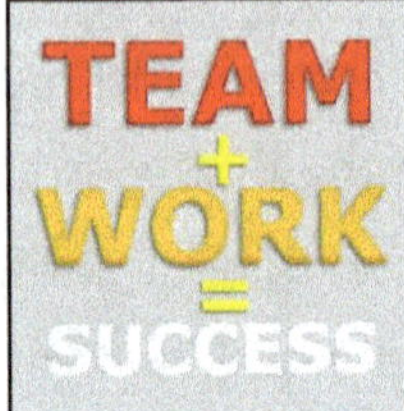

Identify your company's default posture and review it at each roll call.

I always tried to focus on what I called my company's default posture and roll call is a great time to review this with the members working the tour. The default posture is:

- We are going to a fire today.
- We will default to an aggressive mindset regardless of the strategy.
- We will find a victim inside every fire we respond to, and we will have a plan of what to do when we find them.
- If we find one victim, there will be more victims.

Let's look at each of these in a little more detail.

Very few firefighters work for departments that go to working structure fires on a regular basis. Most firefighters belong to either suburban or rural departments and can go for several months without "catching a job." On the career side, through shift schedules and time off, several months can extend out even further.

To paraphrase the laws of learning, what you have done most recently is what you will do the best. If you have been making EMS runs and automatic fire alarms for the last several months, your performance at a working fire can suffer. This is why I always liked to say to my people at roll call that we were going to make a fire today. I wanted to get their attention; I wanted them to start thinking about our actions before we were dispatched. I wanted to get Joe the Landscaper to leave his side job alone and start thinking about the fire job. I know what some are saying, well, that is all well and good, but what if you don't make a fire? Doesn't that take away from the impact of your statement?

As Jocko Willink would say, "We didn't make a fire today. Good. Just more time to get ready for when we do."

It has been said that the term "aggressive" is really about doing things the right way. Whatever the situation is, I want to get ahead of the problem and stop the loss. I don't advocate taking unreasonable risk for property that is lost, but there is value in property, and I think we have an obligation to save as much as we can. Often, people slow down when they hear the incident is going defensive. A defensive fire deserves the same amount of aggression as an offensive fire; it's just a little more complicated. In most commercial occupancies, the stock is insured so that loss will be covered. If we can aggressively attack a defensive fire and save the building, the owner can return more rapidly to operation, and there is a higher chance that they will remain in our jurisdiction.

If we write off the building because we are going defensive, statistics tell us that there is a good chance the business will not re-establish itself in our jurisdiction. They will take their insurance payout and go find a jurisdiction that is offering tax abatements. There are few departments that can lose assets of their tax base. Even in a worst-case scenario, saving a small part of a building might result in saving the business owner's records or maybe their computer servers. Is it not our role to help those who are victims of fire in any way we can?

Expecting victims and having a plan for what to do when you find them is just another way of saying we need to do our job the right way. There are countless examples of people being rescued from buildings where at first glance you would think there is no way someone could still be alive in there. As for the plan, it depends a lot on your staffing and company assignment. For a truck company or a rescue company, things are pretty much cut and dry. Find the victim and remove them via the shortest route from the hazardous atmosphere.

For an engine company things are a little different. Kyle Romagus of the Smooth Bore Cartel suggests a plan where the nozzle firefighter stays with the nozzle, and the other members remove the victim. I am not saying this is the only way, but it makes a lot of sense to me. However, you decide to handle this situation, don't wait until you find a victim in a smoky hallway to start your decision-making.

Finding a victim is a challenging situation; finding multiple victims increases the challenges tenfold. Think about all the runs you have made in the last month and how many of them were to a dwelling or structure that housed more than one person? If we acknowledge the possibility, then we have the obligation to figure out how we will deal with the situation. Granted, you might not have what would be considered enough personnel on the fireground. I say you must play the hand you are dealt.

The key here is to have personnel who can remove a victim and get back into the fight and/or a system where the location of the victim can be identified as the starting point for the continuation of the search. If your nozzle person is still inside, putting water on the fire is a pretty easy starting point. If you are operating as a truck or a squad and don't have a nozzleman holding a position, then maybe you leave a tool or a box light to mark the location where you found the victim.

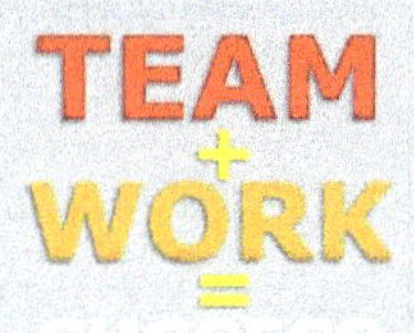

The key is to have personnel who can remove a victim and get back into the fight and a system where the location of the victim can be identified as the starting point for the continuation of the search.

Regardless of the method, having an agreed-upon method that everyone knows will make continuing the search effective. Whatever method you decide on, make sure the surrounding companies know what to look for if they are the ones to continue the search. The front yard of a working fire is not the place to figure this whole operation out.

The military uses a concept called first line, second line, and third line equipment that can be very helpful to us. First line gear is what you carry on your person and in your gear. Good teams pay attention to this. I have seen fire officers ask their members "Does anyone have something to write with?" Without saying it this officer said they weren't really prepared. In terms of what you should have on your person I expected my folks to have something to write with and on. They should carry their Driver's license, and their EMT or Paramedic card. Some states require a valid CPR card for your EMT or Paramedic license to be in compliance. A watch is a good thing to have, and with all the relevant apps nowadays, it seems like a cell phone is almost a necessity. A little cash is a handy thing to have just in case. I am a fan of a good knife and a multi-tool, but these items lean more to personal preference.

In terms of what should be first gear in your bunker gear, boy, this question is always good to start a full throttle conversation. I like to be as light and lean as possible. A good pair of wire cutters (another topic for a great firehouse kitchen table debate), a short piece of webbing, a pick-off strap with two non-locking carabiners, and a short piece of utility rope are on my short list of must-haves. A mega-mover cut in half with the cut end sealed in duct tape isn't a bad idea either. It will come in handy when you find that naked, unconscious fire victim with third-degree burns. To keep things simple, I like to keep one item per pocket to avoid the easter egg hunt because I have so much stuff in my pockets.

Second line gear would be those things you wear directly underneath or on top of your bunker gear. For me, underneath means my portable radio in a holster with a radio strap. There are a lot of opinions about this, and sometimes it just comes down to what you prefer. I will say that I have read the report from Captain Bowen's LODD, and one of the recommendations is that the use of lapel mics, radio holsters, and straps become policy for the Asheville Fire Department.

On top of my bunker gear refers to my SCBA, my box light, and if assigned, a thermal imager. When you set your gear up, adjust your SCBA straps so a slight tug will tighten the straps to your desired fit. Sometimes, when the straps are all the way out, they can be difficult to adjust. Also, by taking some of the slack out of the straps you end up with more of the strap to grab to make that final adjustment. Check your SCBA with it on your back. This way, everything will be in the position it will be in at a fire. You are hardwiring the neural pathways about locating the controls of your SCBA. If you get caught in a Mayday these neural pathways will become very important.

The other important point about your SCBA is that full is full. 4300 is not full for a 4500 psi cylinder. 200 PSI can give you as much as 20 additional breaths. Do not shortchange yourself. The exertion of moving a 300-pound fire victim might require those couple of extra breaths.

Box lights are a great help, but you should wear them in a way that you can remove them in an entanglement and get them on the floor out in front of you to help search when smoke conditions are not down to the floor. The statistics of how many times firefighters fail to take the thermal imaging camera (TIC) with them are staggering. The TIC used correctly can aid in search, both for fire and victims, and firefighter survival. Why do you want to go into a fight and leave an asset behind?

The third line gear is the equipment that goes along with your riding position. Take a few minutes and make sure everything is squared away. If you make a run an hour after shift change, it is too late to find out that the house load is fouled. I remember one time going to my volunteer firehouse for drill night and finding the cross-lays loaded in a manner that made it almost impossible to effectively deploy the lines. Guess the duty crews weren't checking the rig too carefully. I would also add that if you are an hour into your shift, you now own the problem! You can blame the outgoing shift all you want, but you've been on duty for an hour, and when the train goes off the tracks, the bosses are only going to ask, "You've been here for an hour, why didn't you fix it?"

Good companies look at the issues of workspace and workflow. What are the critical tools you are more than likely to need at a working fire? A good example is the pre-connects of an engine company. If it looks good, it will pull good. If the load looks like a mess of spaghetti, fix it!

I know, I know the off going platoon shouldn't have left it like that. When I hear a member say that I always ask them to tell me about their last perfect shift. Maybe that off coming platoon made a bunch of runs, they did an unsuccessful CPR job on a small child and repacked the hose after a room and contents fire in the rain at 0300. There is nothing wrong with extending a little grace to the other members assigned to your firehouse.

We are all human, and someday you are very likely to do the same thing. If this is a recurring issue, make sure your officer knows about it and let him/her take care of the matter. Now take a couple of minutes to repack the line and get ready for the next fire. We can use this concept to apply to any type of company and any riding position. I see a lot of fire departments using inventory sheets and they are fine for accountability, but in that first hour I want to make sure my primary equipment is battle ready.

Starting the day off with a quick drill is a good way to get everyone focused for the tour. It could be nothing more than stretching a line, throwing a ladder, or tagging a plug. A quick drill is a great way to get everyone together and focused on the mission. The basics are what makes or breaks an incident and are well suited for a quick review and drill at the start of a tour. I am not talking about anything that is long and complicated with a multi-page lesson plan. By drilling in the first hour, we send a message that training is important and is something we will commit to every day. The quick drills are a great way to get everyone in the company involved.

I believe officers play a critical role in training, but they shouldn't be the only ones playing a role. The type of drills I am talking about should be able to be led by anyone in the company from the senior man or woman to the newest probie. I like to focus on the tasks that will be required in the first five minutes of a working fire. Forcing doors, stretching lines, and throwing ladders are all good topics for your first hour quick drills.

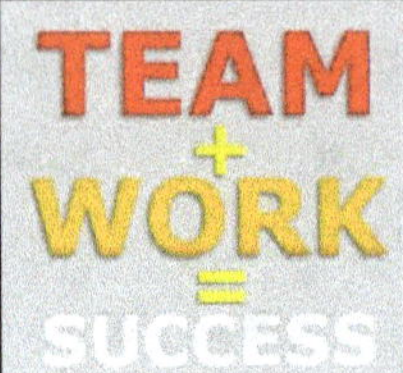

The most important thing: Spend time together. You cannot build a strong team from behind the closed doors of individual bunk rooms.

The last thing, and it could be argued as the most important thing, is to spend a little time together. You cannot build a strong team from behind the closed doors of individual bunk rooms. Sitting around the kitchen table and just talking with each other can go a long way. I often use the metaphor of "Joe the landscaper." This is the guy who has a landscaping business on the side. He seldom works overtime and tends to be quiet and keeps to himself. He's not a bad firefighter, but he is not a great one either.

Right now, a lot of you are probably drawing a mental picture of our friend Joe and it isn't too flattering. By spending some time together at the start of shift we find out that Joe's wife is homeschooling three children, one of whom is special needs. Joe's oldest is in their third year of college without any scholarships. Two of the three kids that Joe's wife is homeschooling are twins who will be graduating high school in two years and heading off to college. Joe doesn't get a free pass; he is still expected to meet our standards, but learning a little about Joe, maybe we see him in a different light.

Maybe our opinions get tempered because of his situation. Maybe we get a new understanding of Joe and why he is the way he is. This information isn't going to just drop into our laps; the information comes to us because we spend some time with each other.

Roll call gives the officer a chance to check in on everyone, review important information and set the tone for the day.
Five minutes here will pay dividends for the remainder of the tour.

Chapter Nuggets

- Roll call is a chance to check in with all your assigned members to make sure everyone is battle-ready.
- Reinforce your default posture at roll call so everyone knows exactly what the mission is.
- The default posture:
    - We are going to a fire today!
    - Regardless of the strategy, we will employ an aggressive application of our chosen tactics.
    - We will find a victim at every structure fire, and when we do, we have a plan on what to do.
    - If there is one victim, there will be more.
- Your first line gear is what you carry on your person, your second line gear is what you wear over your bunker gear, your third line gear is the equipment assigned to your riding position.
- Start the day off with a quick drill.
- Spend time in the first hour to build relationships among the team members.

TEAM DYNAMICS

Anytime you put people together in a group working to meet a common goal, there will be what I call "dynamics" that will develop among the members. These dynamics are the way people interact with each other and have a profound impact on the success of the team. If we ignore this fact and think "it will be ok, these things will just sort themselves out," the team will eventually lose. The real problem is when the team dynamics negatively impact the zero-fail environment that is the fireground.

I believe the dynamic between the officer and the members is probably the most important dynamic and the critical element here is respect. In the simplest of terms, the members of a company should be able to say their officer respects them, and they, in turn, respect the officer.

Respect can be a complicated subject. There is respect for the rank, i.e., the boss gives an order the members follow the order. If the order is not illegal, immoral, or unsafe, the members don't really have a choice in the matter.

Failure to follow the order is insubordination, and in some environments, which could be grounds for termination. When talking about respect, I often flashback to a video I saw of the late General Colin Powell. In the clip, General Powell recounts the advice he got as a young officer from a senior Non-Commissioned Officer. The NCO told Powell that he would know when the men truly respected him when they would follow him, if nothing else, out of simple curiosity to see what he was going to do.

Officers who make a constant effort to earn the respect of their members will find it much easier to get their members to follow them than those who don't.

We cannot assume we will automatically get respect just because. The officer who only leans on the trumpets on their collar or the senior member who thinks longevity is enough are in for a rude awakening. As important as trust is, and trust really is the foundation, respect goes hand in hand with trust. Strong teams will go beyond the easy button answer. Are you sensitive to the things that might bother someone in your company? I read a quote that talked about a female firefighter and how uncomfortable she was when her "brothers" started discussing their feelings on a trans woman who was born a male but was now competing as a woman. We all have opinions about what could be considered controversial topics, but based on the composition of your company, is it really necessary to discuss this stuff in the firehouse?

Respect means that you are willing to hit the brakes and consider how your comments will come across to others. People who respect their teammates are willing to look at things from perspectives other than their own.

Respect is a by-product of building relationships. This can be a very difficult road to navigate, especially if you are an officer. As soon as you say "relationships," some people think the conversation is going to go all "touchy feely." There is an element of the "touchy feely" we need not to be afraid to express. I am not saying you need to be best friends with everyone with whom you work. In my career, there were people who very quickly and consistently got on my last nerve. No matter how I personally felt, I realized that for the good of the team, I had to find a way to see value in those people. No matter who or what, if you look hard enough, you will find something in that person you really don't like that might bring value to the emergency scene.

As positive as I try to be there are some folks who will just try your patience to the last second. At times like these one should remember a couple of important points. The first one is one that comes from the ancient Stoics that goes along the lines that the control you have in the universe is how you react to a situation. People can annoy you if you let them and some people make a point to be the squeaky wheel. Maybe when you find yourself in this situation you can count to ten, maybe you excuse yourself and go for a short walk out in the engine room, maybe you just try to smile. They say it's very hard to get mad when you are smiling. I don't have a bullet proof way to manage an adverse reaction to an annoying person, but I will say you have to figure out a coping mechanism that works for you. Left unchecked these little things will add up and can help to produce a toxic firehouse. The other thing to think about is as much as we would hope we could stuff these feelings deep down inside when the bells hit, they will still be there and can negatively impact our performance on a run.

Part of building relationships is getting to know the people on a deeper level. It doesn't hurt to ask simple questions like what's your spouse's name? What are your kids into? What is your least favorite food (so we don't plan a firehouse meal that will not be appreciated)? The little things can translate into a solid foundation for what you are trying to build with your team. Maybe the person's spouse's name is the same as your spouse's. How about that, a simple question led to a commonality between you two. It's not a bad thing to know that one of your co-worker's children is playing travel ball and they just spent their four-day break staying in motels and driving a couple of hundred miles. Even if the team had a horrible outing it is still a nice gesture to show a little interest.

When we are building our team, we must include all our members. Some officers might feel it is important to keep a little distance between themselves, and the members assigned to their command. To an extent, I think there is some merit to this, but we also must remember that officers are human beings too. Maybe the officer is standoffish because they are new to their role and trying to figure out how to navigate the newly given responsibilities. Some of the loneliest times I have had have been as an officer trying to make the transition from buddy to boss.

The companies who isolate themselves from their officers can create a weak spot that will show itself at the worst time. In most instances, there is blame to go all the way around in weak teams. It is very easy to blame the officer in this situation, but if you have not tried to build a bridge, then some of the fault rests with you.

If the officer is lacking when it comes to interpersonal interactions, pick up the ball. Try starting a conversation. Try including the officer in a conversation by asking their opinion. The old saying that we "win as a team and we lose as a team" is very true in the firehouse. Be inclusive of all your members, and the strength of the team will grow by leaps and bounds. If you are going to be an officer, then to an extent, you must develop a little bit of thick skin. As a new officer don't be surprised when a conversation stops when you walk into the room. This might catch you off guard, but it can very well happen.

If you start to take this personally, it can impact the team. Sometimes firefighters will do this to see how you will react, especially if you are new to the company. Does this make you withdraw? Does this make you want to relax your expectations to fit into the group? Do you confront this head-on like a bull in a China shop? My best advice is not to let this bother you and just be yourself. If the conversation stops when you walk into the room, try to start it back up.

Talk about last night's football game, someone's son or daughter who is playing traveling sports, or how about this unique approach - what you are going to train on today. Remember as the officer you have a lot of control over your team's dynamic. As your team matures into the high-performing unit you are striving for, you will start to attract attention. This can be very good and very bad. Some people will see your team as the example to emulate. Others will become jealous. They will blame you for making them look bad and not take responsibility for their shortcomings. What is important is not to let either of these groups deter you from the goal of building and maintaining a high-performing team.

Just because you have a great reputation among your peers does not mean the hard work is over. It has been said that getting into the US Army Ranger Regiment is hard, but it is even harder to stay in the Regiment. We can get exhausted by the work it takes to reach a goal and be tempted to take our foot off the gas. A little rest is ok, but the team needs to appreciate the fact that yesterday's success does not guarantee tomorrow's victory. The officer is ultimately responsible, but in the best teams, anyone who sees something can step up and speak their mind. A big part of team dynamics is knowing exactly how the team got to their level of performance and creating the metrics that can be used to keep the team's razor edge. The specifics can vary greatly, but if you embrace the cultural elements discussed in the chapter about Culture, you will have a foundation for success.

Now it's time to spend a few minutes on the haters. They are out there and mostly jealous because they don't have the drive to do the work themselves to match what you have done. The haters will look for ways to bring you down because they will not work to bring themselves up.

There are two very important points to understand here. The first is that no matter what you do, or where you work, there will be haters. Accepting this reality can be very liberating. Marcus Aurelius is quoted as saying "You have the power over your own mind - not outside events. Realize this and you will find strength." Letting the haters impact you only gives them strength to continue down their path and make your journey more difficult.

The second point is that to be a high-performing team, you must be a solid team together or apart. As an example, one of your members works on an overtime shift at a firehouse filled with haters. When your member shows up for the OT shift, the haters start their game play. They will say things like "Hey, what's it really like working at ______?" or "Just between you and me is working for Captain ______ any fun or is he a real ______?" It is easy to drop your guard and either go along to get along or feelings that really belong back at the company and not an overtime firehouse. Once these things get out, and believe they will, you will find yourself spending a lot of energy defusing the situation. A simple rule to follow, and one that will support team dynamics, is, "we are a strong company together or apart."

A high-performing team places great value on the health and development of its members. Everyone in your firehouse should be part of this and play an active role in making sure all the members are operating at the standard the company has set. This is very important when a new member is assigned to the company. If you have built a solid company, you are probably viewed as a force multiplier. Your firehouse is where people go to master the craft.

Understand that this means that you are likely to get your share of probies. A lot of firefighters don't like this. Probies mean they will have to do some extra work, answer questions, spend less time in the recliner and more time on the drill ground. If you think like this then you are well on the way to being a mediocre firefighter. Take pride in the fact that the administration trusts you with developing the department's new talent. You may become an influential figure to the future chief of the department.

Part of developing our new members is making sure they understand the dynamics of a team-centered environment. I would ask newly assigned members if they were military veterans or had a recent background in playing team sports. If they said no to both questions our starting point will be talking about how to be a successful team member. Firefighting skills will come after this. I have seen countless young firefighters get a bad rap because they didn't fit in.

Sometimes it is squarely on the shoulders of the young firefighters because they felt entitled or they were too lazy to do the work. In a lot of cases, the new firefighters just didn't understand the team environment. They didn't realize that the group takes precedence over the individual. They didn't know that everyone had a role and we are all depending on everyone else to do their part. They didn't know that there would be standards and expectations, and that if you did not live up to these requirements, you were being disrespectful to the team.

All these seem so self-explanatory, but to some people they aren't. You cannot expect someone to master their craft if they don't understand the context in which they will apply their skills. These points are critical for healthy team dynamics and even if a new member has a strong team background it will not hurt to throw these few items into one of your first conversations.

Team dynamics can be positive or negative. The dynamics your team embodies will impact everything you do. If having a high-performing team is your goal, spend some time making sure you address the components of team dynamics.

Chapter Nuggets

- High-performing teams understand how important the dynamic between members is to the overall success of the team.
- In high-performing teams, the members respect their officer, and the officer respects the members.
- High-performing teams are a strong group even when they are apart and will not allow outsiders to drive a wedge into their team.
- High-performing teams take responsibility for the development of their members.

TRAINING

High-performing teams understand the value of training. They realize that success on the fireground has a direct connection to the effort they put into their training. Not only does this emphasis on training produce positive impacts at an emergency, but it is also one of things that attracts and retains the high performers.

You cannot have a high-performing team without a good training ethic.

Many firefighters think that training must be some type of extravagant, five-page lesson plan production. This is anything but accurate. One of the tenets of quality training is an exchange of information where the one who receives the information understands the concept and importance. A 20-minute talk in the apparatus bay might be more beneficial to a probationary firefighter than a four-hour "death by PowerPoint." There are times when a deep dive into a subject is necessary, but there is value anytime information is passed.

This goes back to the old quality vs. quantity argument so don't put barriers in the way of training. Saying that you do not have the time to train is a poor excuse that doesn't really hold water. When people tell me they don't have time to do this or that I always ask to see their phones and look at their scrolling history, I think you get my point.

Officers need to be very aware of the attitude they take toward training and the impact it has. High-performing teams embrace the need for quality training as a fundamental part of their culture. Officers who use training as either a reward or a punishment are doing considerable damage to the team. No matter how motivated a person is, they will be affected by their surroundings. High performers at some point will lose the desire to improve if their environment is not one that encourages continuous improvement. Training is the key element for this upward trajectory, but if leadership is not encouraging training and just using it as a tool to manage the workplace, that attitude will at some point be adopted by the members. A good way to kill a high-performing team is to not respect the role that training plays.

You can't really have a good discussion about training without defining what you want the training to produce. I understand that some training is designed for a very specific purpose and does not necessarily transfer to the fire ground. Your yearly required harassment training, right to know, and other mandated topics are not what I am talking about.

I am talking about the training your team uses to prepare for the emergency scene. Some organizations look at the number of hours their members spend on training. This might fulfill some legal requirements or mandates, but a quantitative approach does not guarantee success on the fireground. Certifications do indicate a level of performance but there are issues associated with just chasing certifications. It is common to hear the term minimum standard when discussing the pass point for issuing a certification. I will say that the minimum standard is one step above unacceptable, and I question if that is the approach we should use in a high-threat endeavor. My expectation for training is that it will produce tough competent firefighters who are able to operate at an extremely high level of proficiency in challenging, dangerous environments.

One of the most important things to remember when delivering training to produce the end state that I have just described is that the fight is always won by the basics. Top-performing teams understand this concept, and they dedicate a tremendous amount of time and resources to honing their basic skill set. Most professional sports teams employ numerous position coaches who specialize in a very specific part of their sport. It is said that the US Army's Special Missions Unit is one of the best combat marksmen in the world, and when you watch any podcast with one of these soldiers, they always remark that their success is a byproduct of the time they spend refining the basics of combat shooting. If you want your team to win, you must put a high priority on excellence in the basics and not let the shiny butterflies detract from this pursuit.

Working with high performers requires more than just saying this is what we are going to do. Smart people are always going to ask the dreaded "why" question, and if you don't have a good answer for them, your ability to influence and lead will fade. Sets and reps are the only way to hardwire the body's neural pathways for an action, task, or skill to become instinctive and reflexive. The more we do a specific task, the more myelin the body produces, which increases the speed of transmission for the impulses that allow the task to be completed. There is no easy button here, if you want to be fast you have got to spend the time building these pathways. Speed on the fireground, as Ben Schulatz says, is our weapon when time is our enemy and this is a great answer to the why question.

When operating in a high-risk/high-threat environment like the fireground, the human mind works along three planes: the conscious, the subconscious, and the self-image. Science clearly tells us that we cannot multitask in the conscious mind. Where we get a huge tactical advantage is moving manipulative tasks from the conscious to the subconscious mind.

For example, once I decide to put on my SCBA, if I have built the neural pathways, I don't think about the steps needed to don the SCBA. Through sets and reps in training, this task is transferred to the subconscious mind. Now I can use my conscious mind to size up the scene, look for cues, develop strategies, and decide on tactics.

Training in the form of sets and reps is the key, and only through quality and continuous training will we be able to develop this transfer of skills from the conscious to the subconscious mind. This "transfer process," as I call it, allows us to move more rapidly through the OODA loop, thus increasing our efficiency and reducing our time to target. The OODA Loop is a concept developed by Colonel James Boyd that basically says those who can move through a cycle of Observing, Orienting, Deciding, and Acting quicker than their opponent will win a fight. Our endeavor is called firefighting, and the OODA Loop concept applies to us just like it applies to fighter pilots who used it to achieve superiority over their opponents. When someone in your company asks why we are doing the same old task training repeatedly, you now have an answer that is backed by science.

The "transfer process" can be a valuable tool to increasing efficiency on the fireground, but you must define what skills you want to focus on, so the process actually occurs. I know some people will roll their eyes when I mention the NFPA, but there is value you can find in the 1010 standard, Standard on Professional Qualifications for Firefighters. I do not think this standard is the end-all, be-all, but your path to excellence must start somewhere, and this is a good starting point. You can use this standard to identify what the key performance skills are for the members of your team. Once you have these standards, you can go to work on enhancing the abilities of your members in performing the skills.

There is value to having an industry standard and like it or not the NFPA is our industry standard. If there are things in the standard that you think are not in the best interest of effective training, apply to get on the committee and work to change it.

Training to a standard takes the guesswork and the subjectivity out of the picture. When I was the Chief in Sunrise Beach, Missouri, I wanted an objective means to evaluate the performance of our companies. We started conducting basic company evolutions at our training facility. As an example, how long did it take for an engine company to stretch a 200-foot 1¾ pre-connect? The evolution started when the air brakes were applied and ended when the company was masked up, line charged, ready to break the IDLH threshold. We ended up with a time of 1 minute and 34 seconds.

Now as the officers train their people, they know what good looks like. They have a standard to measure their performance, and the standard has true fireground applicability. It is hard to argue that the faster you can deploy a line and be ready to enter a structure is not a good thing for an engine company to be able to accomplish. Having a standard, be it from the NFPA 1010 or your internal company performance drills, allows you to train with a purpose.

As is often the case when we were working on our company evolutions, there were some second and third-order effects. Second and third order effects are things that happen that are not the primary effect the task was designed to produce. We would video some of the companies as they were going through the evolution and after the exercise, we all watched the video. One of our firefighters named Tim could be seen having some difficulty at one point. As we watched the video, and before anyone else could say something, Tim acknowledged the problem areas and made a comment about how he could knock several seconds off his company's time. I know this chapter is about training, but this is also an example of trust and security in the team.

Tim could have sat back and hoped no one would bring up his shortcomings. Because he trusted the members of his team, and we embraced a learning and teaching culture, Tim did not shy away from ownership. Remember that everything is interconnected in the firehouse, and when people trust and support each other, positive second and third-order effects happen. Now back to our conversation about training.

If we agree that training is critical to fireground performance, then we should have a validated way to determine the critical tasks that deserve attention on the company's training schedule. One method that gets all your team members involved is what I call *"Our Ten."* To establish Our Ten, get all your members to list the ten things they think your company must master.

If you are assigned to an engine company, throwing a 35 ft extension ladder probably will not find its way into your list. Once everyone makes their list simply compare the list. When you see an item that appears on multiple lists, that is an item that probably deserves some attention. This method could also bring to light something you just don't think about. Everyone has a different lens through which they see the world, and this could add a valuable drill to your training schedule that you might not otherwise have thought about.

The *"Our Ten"* method also helps create buy-in for your company's training program. Everyone has been given a chance to express what they think is important for company success. Now, when it's time to drill, the drill is not just what the boss says; it is what at least one member of the company identified as a critical task.

The strongest, highest-performing teams will, at some point, struggle with motivation. We are working with people not robots and it is unrealistic to think at some point someone will question the need to train on a particular topic. By soliciting the input of all your members, the training program becomes a joint decision not just what the boss sees as important.

So now that we have identified the basic firefighting skills needed by our members and the 10 specific tasks at which our team needs to be proficient, what's next? I think there is real value in having a training schedule.

A schedule does a lot of things. First, when you put pen to paper, you are demonstrating to your team that you value training. You are committing the most precious resource, your time, to training. I have seen countless times when a company's training is done on the spur of the moment. There is no more importance associated with this approach as there is with emptying the trash cans. By posting a training schedule, your team members are more likely to be prepared for your drill.

One of Thorndike's Laws of Learning is the Law of Readiness. Thorndike says that people are more likely to learn when they are ready to engage in a learning activity. Knowing that our company is going to drill at a certain time on a certain day helps set the stage for true learning to occur. You might be surprised to see some of your team members spending some time refreshing their skills prior to a future drill.

The members know what is coming, and high performers have a sense of pride in their chosen field. They don't want to look bad in front of the other team members, so they just might brush the cobwebs off before a drill. Sharing the training schedule with your members is a win when building that high-performing team you want.

Some people might say that any training is good training, but I don't agree with that statement. Training that creates training scars is detrimental to the team's performance. If you allow shortcuts on the drill ground, don't be surprised when they show up on the fireground. I am not saying every drill must be in full PPE, but if you are doing a drill that requires full PPE, then that is what everyone needs to be wearing. As a senior staff member, I dropped in on a multi-company exercise. The drill involved deploying multiple hand lines, and I watched as an acting officer pulled and operated a line while not wearing their gloves. When I brought this to the attention of the chief running the drill, he didn't think it was a big deal. The problem is twofold.

First, by not correcting that member, we are saying that this behavior is OK, and the chance of that behavior finding its way to the fireground increases. I have always said, learn how to perform fireground tasks while wearing your gloves. If you adopt this mindset in training, it will follow you to the fireground. This takes some work, but once you become comfortable operating with your gloves on, there will be no reason to take them off. The other problem with this example is everyone sees everything. If you want bad behaviors to show up on the fireground, allow them in training. Everyone who saw this issue not being addressed was given the green light to do the same thing.

At some point the leaders must be leaders and ensure that we don't allow training scars to become acceptable behaviors.

If the desired end state of training is enhanced performance on the fireground, then we must understand the different types of practice. In his book, *Going Pro*, Tony Kern speaks about the different types of practice. Naive practice is just going out and practicing. There is no preparation, no standards against which to measure success, no metrics used to measure performance, and no feedback given to the individual engaging in the practice. It is "naive" to think that this type of practice will have any beneficial results. When I first started playing golf, I was totally self-taught. I read a book and then went to the driving range. I could hit a ball straight for about 10 ft. The more I practiced, the worse I got.

It wasn't until my wife paid for lessons with a professional that I started to see some improvement. The improvement came after the pro undid all the bad habits and techniques I picked up while engaging in naive practice. It is very hard to be objective about your own performance while you are physically engaged in a task. Deliberate practice involves training to a standard, using metrics to gauge improvement, and feedback from a knowledgeable person who can watch and evaluate your performance. Deliberate practice is what will enhance emergency scene operations.

Deliberate practice isn't just for the less senior members of your team. The fireground does not care about how many years you have on the job or how many fires you have had. Sooner or later, the only way to come out on the winning end is to seek constant improvement.

High-performing teams understand this, and they demand that every member of the team must be open to coaching. There is a lot of ego that comes with being a firefighter, but the drill ground is one place that you need to leave your ego back at the firehouse. The newest member of your company just might know a new technique that will allow you to be a little more efficient. That new member might notice something in your technique that can be improved, thus making the overall team better.

Visual feedback is very beneficial when working with people to improve technique or performance. I can tell you about corrections you should make, but when you can see exactly what I am saying, learning increases. Think about how much film a professional football player watches in a week getting ready for game day. The number is easily in double digits.

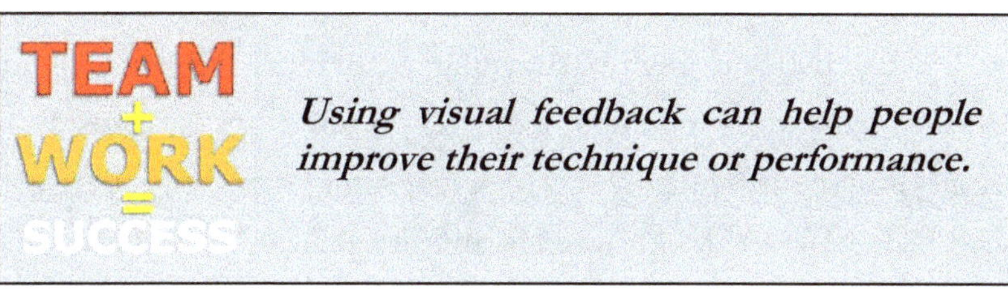

Using visual feedback can help people improve their technique or performance.

We can use the same technique to help our members get better. The next time you head out to the drill ground, use your phone to record the training. For less than twenty bucks, you can buy a cable that will allow you to play your video back on the station TV. Now everyone can see everything. I must say that if you are going to use this technique, the boss needs to be the boss. This isn't about showing people up or letting the wolves eat their own. This is about allowing your people to have direct feedback to improve performance and enhance fireground efficiency. Done properly, this technique can be a real game changer.

The other thing that I will say is if the culture and atmosphere among the team is correct, people will want to see the video of their performance. They want to know exactly where they need to do some work. In the right culture everyone accepts the fact that no one is perfect, and there is always room for improvement. What is really amazing and I have seen this with my own two eyes is, in the right culture the people who are the subject of the video will often point out their mistakes before anyone else has a chance to do so and they tend to be their own worst critics. Using video is an excellent tool for building that true learning culture in your team.

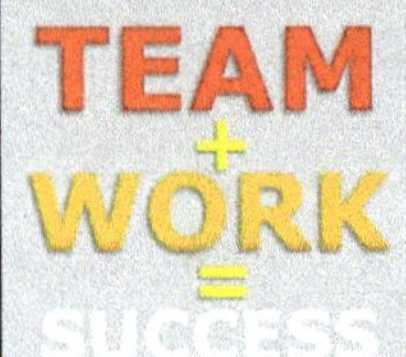

Demanding training will test a member's ability to remain calm and focused when completing a task

To build a high-performing team for the fireground, realistic, demanding training is a must. I do not dispute the need for classroom-type instruction. To be a true subject matter expert you need to have both the knowledge and the skills. Our communities deserve nothing less. Without naming names, we all know of training programs that are computer-based, check-the-box type training. These programs are very good at what they do, providing and tracking mandated subject material. They come up very short on building fireground capabilities. By demanding training, I mean training that will test a member's ability to remain calm and focus on completing a task, but caution must be used. There is a big difference between demanding training and putting your people through a "suck fest."

As a young firefighter, I always dreaded going to confidence-building training. Back in my day this was code for "we are going to make you very uncomfortable just for the sake of it." Often, those running the drills were in their station uniforms, sitting in the shade, watching us struggle. We have all been there and know what this is like. The big problem with this approach is that it does nothing to truly build fireground skills and often puts a sour taste in one's mouth for training.

To avoid the problems described above, there are some simple rules to follow. First off, whatever skills will be tested in the demanding training session should be well within the capability of the members and have been practiced extensively prior to the exercise. If the skills that must be employed in the training are not skills which the members are very competent with, the training becomes an exercise in survival with little long-term benefit. Skill acquisition must occur before skill mastery and the introduction of stressors into the training.

The second point to consider is that demanding training should be a progressive endeavor. Do not go from zero to one hundred in a two-hour drill. Turn up the intensity of the training gradually so the members can hone their skills and build a sense of competence.

The third point is to not build in any of the "I gotcha you" details. Challenges are OK, but they should have some relatability to the real world. Have you ever seen an instructor hide a manikin during a search drill in a way that is highly unlikely for the search team to find? When the drill is over, this instructor makes a point about how the team missed a victim. All this does is stroke the instructor's ego and demoralize the search team. I am not saying make things easy, I am saying make demanding training that makes sense. Hiding a baby manikin in a microwave oven is not my idea of effective training but I am willing to bet some instructors will do that just to make a nonsensical point.

Good training is the lifeblood of high-performing teams. You must invest time and energy to develop your team's ability to perform. The fireground does not bargain. Either you show up prepared, or you don't; the consequences of not being prepared are paid at a very high price. Your job as a member of a high-performing team is to make sure you don't have to pay that price.

Chapter Nuggets

- Quality training is an absolute necessity for high-performing teams.
- The boss's attitude toward training is critical for success; training should never be a reward or punishment.
- Define what you want the end state of training to be before you start training.
- Be able to articulate the "why" behind the training
- Involve all your team members in deciding the team's training.
- Put pen to paper and publish a training schedule. This will enhance accountability and keep everyone on track.
- Use guided practice and feedback to make sure your training is effective.

MINDSET

General Mattis once said that "the most important six inches on the battlefield is the space between every Marine's ears." I could not agree more with that statement. How you look at things will shape how your team performs. Every member of the team must understand this because we all have an impact on the team's overall performance. Over the course of five decades, here are some of the mindset tools I have found to be quite valuable.

I used to get very annoyed when I heard firefighters referred to as public servants. It seemed to me that the term servant was demeaning at best. I wasn't there to be anyone's servant; I was a hometown hero, the public adored me, and little children wanted to grow up and be just like me. What do you notice about the last few sentences? There are a lot of I's mentioned and nothing about them. When I started to really think about the reason behind being a firefighter, it occurred to me that to be part of the fire service, you are expected to serve. This shift in perspective was huge.

Now I realize that every day in the firehouse was about the people I got to serve. The privilege of being part of the fire service was bestowed upon me because I was willing to serve them. As I was promoted, I became aware of how important it was to be a servant leader.

We have all worked for those officers who don't embrace the concept of servant leadership, and my bet is that those years spent under the thumb of these officers were probably the longest and least rewarding years. If we want our personnel to have the mindset that will produce a high-performing team, we must emphasize that our role is to serve others. If we don't get this right, the chances of getting anything else right are greatly reduced.

From the time I was a young firefighter, I always tried to have a sense of ownership for the area I was assigned. I wanted to "own the local." I didn't want anyone to take a run that belonged to my company, and certainly no one was going to beat me into our runs. I strongly believe the saying "it's not our emergency" should be banned from every firehouse, and the person who coined the phrase should be severed from the fire service. Of course, it's our emergency. The people calling us have found themselves in a situation that is beyond their capability to handle, and the fire service are the ones they have turned to for help. It is our job to restore a sense of safety and stability to their lives. By taking ownership of our locals, we begin to see the callers in a different light.

I looked at the people who lived across from Station 3 in Durham, North Carolina, not as citizens or customers, but as the firehouse's neighbors. Sure, it was annoying sometimes when the kids came in when we were busy, but we always tried to keep the bay doors up when the weather was nice. I began to realize that the firehouse bay was a safe place for kids who didn't have a lot of safe places in their lives. I began to recognize the people in the neighborhood. I learned that the elderly couple right around the corner from the firehouse were pretty much shut ins.

That got me thinking about what I would do if we responded to their house at 0300 and there were smoke-stained windows and evidence of a working fire. This got me to start really paying attention to window sizes, identifying rooms from the exterior, thinking how I was going to deploy a handline through the fence and clutter in the front yard. I am not saying you should adopt the mindset that I had and I am sure there are some very good firefighters who don't see things this way.

What I am saying is this is a tool that might help you and your team. A good process is likely to produce a good end state. My mental and identifying their bedroom from the street. My ability to stretch a hand line improved greatly by thinking about how I would overcome the obstacles in their yard.

When I was promoted, this train of thought really became part of how I lead my company. This is our local, we own it and it is our job to take care of our neighbors. We know the layout of the local better than anyone else. We know the traffic patterns; we know when we can use the main roads and when traffic dictates taking the back roads. We know the numbering system on the streets and after enough time and study, we don't need the communications center to tell us the cross streets. We already know them just from hearing the address. Does this have an effect? I don't know, maybe it saves us a couple of seconds getting out of the firehouse. Maybe the couple of seconds we save are the lost couple of seconds one of our neighbors has before they take their last breath. When we start asking the questions that we can't answer for sure, don't we have a moral obligation to error on the most beneficial side for the victim?

As a Battalion Chief in Cherry Hill, my chief's buggy had a pass key that would allow me access to the roof of an 18-story high-rise apartment building. Occasionally, I would go up to the roof and look out over the city. From this vantage point, I could see just about everything in our city. I would spend a little time thinking about my role and the responsibilities I had for the people who lived in our community. It was common on a summer weekend for the headquarters staff to be "down at the shore." If anything happened, and serious incidents happen all the time when you put 78,000 people in 22 square miles, I was the one everyone was going to look to for solutions.

I believe a few moments of reflection, such as these, can help you achieve and maintain the mindset needed for the responsibilities we have. Simple things like taking ownership help us improve the quality of the service we deliver. Some people might dismiss this line of thinking and that's OK. I don't profess to have the best way; I have a way. My quiet time at the top of the Landmark I Building helped me embrace the ownership I felt in my position. This helped provide and maintain the drive I felt was needed to build a high-performing team. You must find a way you can internalize this feeling of ownership. If it is not genuine, the high performers will see right through it. I will say that high performers recognize quality service when they see it and that is where they want to belong.

The truth of the matter is that there are runs that we just don't want to make. The 3:00 A.M. lift assist to the house you have already been to what seems like a hundred times doesn't really inspire us to do our best work. The bottom line is we don't get to choose what runs we make and what ones we can refuse. When people call 9-1-1 they expect a consistent level of professionalism to show up and solve their problems. It is not our role or right to determine if this run is actually an emergency. If we want to catch the working jobs, making the lift run at 3:00 A.M. is the price for admission. I don't think this is an easy outlook to adopt and at some point, we will all roll our eyes and say "not again" when we recognize the frequent flyer address. This is the point when the high-performing team disciplines itself.

Someone on the team should step up. Someone has to say, "hey it's all just part of the job." Someone has to say, "Hey, it's cool, just hang in the rig, I will take the lead on this one." The old saying that the strength of the wolf is in the pack is the mindset high performing teams understand. We can all have a bad day; we just can't all have the bad day at the same time.

One way you can help manage the frustration of the frequent flyer is what I call "leave it at the door." The team has adopted a turn out standard that says when a run comes in no matter what the address is we turn out in no more than x number of seconds. This is the standard we live by, and it is non-negotiable. The team can say whatever they want when the run is dispatched all the way to the location, but once we arrive, we act as the professionals we say we are. We treat the people who called us just like they were a family member and give them the care and attention we would want a family member to receive. Once we walk out the door, we leave the call and our feelings there. The call is over, we did our job and now is the time to focus on the next run, whatever that might be. This is not always an easy thing to do, but when we operate as a team, someone can remind us to "leave it at the door."

High performing teams avoid at all costs the "well, that's the way we have always done it here" mindset. This attitude does several harmful things. When we say that, we discourage innovation. If this way works, why should I look to do it differently?

Change for the sake of change does not help the team, but we limit our true potential when we are not willing to expand our knowledge and skills. If you have been in the fire service for any amount of time, you know that our battle space and the tools we have available are different from they were ten years ago. By being rigid in our beliefs, we can deny our members' abilities that could save their lives or the lives of the people we are trying to rescue. If you look hard enough, you will find instructors who, to this very day, will tell new firefighters not to flow water on smoke, and we know from all the research and the truly knowledgeable people in the fire service that this is a dangerous and possibly fatal concept. The way we have always done it is not the mindset you find in performing teams.

Another problem with the above mindset is it shuts the less senior people down. The unspoken part of the statement is to keep your opinions to yourself. I don’t want to hear them. You might not actually think this way, but part of being a good team member is thinking about how your words will be interpreted by others. Our new members come to a firehouse with a blank slate. They are not invested in the way it’s always been. They see things that we no longer notice, they have life experiences that we might not have, and they have been exposed to knowledge via their training or the internet that are foreign to us. I am not saying that we shouldn’t expect these folks to earn their seat at the table, everyone needs to work every day to earn their seat. I am also not saying we automatically take everything at face value.

Before we change battle-tested tactics, the new way must be vetted. A good idea in one firehouse might not work in another firehouse. Being critical does not mean you are not open; in fact, the high-performing teams understand that both these characteristics are necessary for success.

Sometimes it is not the message, but how the message is transmitted and/or interpreted. When we say we need to change the way we are doing something, some people will take this as if we are saying they are wrong. This can be a natural reaction and can lead to a lot of conflict. If we look back at our workplace history most of us can relate to a time when our delivery caused this type of conflict. I sure can, and it created some big problems for me.

The most damaging effect when this happens is that it can transfer over to the fireground. Anytime there is negative friction in a team, performance will suffer. If we really care about getting the most out of our team, then we need to have concern for our people. As you begin your discussions about this new concept or technique, it doesn't hurt to acknowledge how some members might react. The simple statement of "I am not saying we are doing something wrong, I am just saying this could be a tool to make us better." If you push too hard you can alienate some members of your team and lose the opportunity to influence the direction of the team.

Acknowledging how some might react is an important step in the change process, but there are two other things to consider. I think the most important thing to remember is that the person who is championing the change must remain open to the possibility that their idea might not work. Some things look very good conceptually but come up short on the fireground. Take the new tactic or equipment to the drill ground and put the watch on it. As I have already discussed, your team should have some time standard benchmarks. If your idea doesn't move the performance needle in a positive direction, then stay with what you know works. No harm, no foul, the drill ground is the palace where we can try, fail and then fix. There is a saying that the master has failed more times than the amateur has attempted.

High-performing teams embrace efforts that are grounded in seeking improvement, even if sometimes they don't work. The second thing to remember is that the new idea is not cast in stone. If, after drilling and discussion, this doesn't work, the team can just revert to the existing practice.

As you meet the challenging questions head-on, you must also think about the possibility that those who resisting are too lazy to do the work required. Adopting new procedures, using new equipment, or changing the way a company operates takes hard work. As much as you need to be sensitive to the other members of the team, you also need to be willing to throw the BS flag.

If people are resisting change because of the work required, the leaders of the team, formal and informal, need to step up and be leaders. You should only discount the new because it doesn't work and the only way to know that for sure is to try and drill. The TV schedule should not dictate the daily schedule, and high-performing teams are perfectly fine with this. If you have built a strong team, then this probably will not be a problem for you. If you are in the process of building a team, be aware that some of your members might not be the most ambitious.

Hand in glove with the "it's the way we have always done it" mindset is the "it will not happen here" mindset. These are the words often heard in firehouses after a LODD or a fatality fire. The truth is that anything can happen anywhere. If your team doesn't have standards and strong leadership, a faulty alarm systems and medical runs can allow complacency to creep in. If you see a fireground going south, then there is a good chance complacency is involved. The high performing teams know that Murphy, the if can go wrong it will go wrong guy, has a seat on the rig every time it makes a run. It is natural to let your guard down when there has been a lull in fire duty. The high-performing teams make sure that someone is always on point and that someone keeps everyone else dialed in. Where high performing teams outshine the others is the role of team gatekeeper moves among all the team members. The team is not dependent on the officer all the time because the officer is just like everyone else, a human being.

Complacency comes to all of us at some time. The officer is bound to have an off day where they will say to themselves this will not happen here and that opens the door for complacency to show up. When this happens someone on the team steps up and says I might not have trumpets on my collar but it's time for me to lead. When the officer of a non-high-performing team has an off day, the other members don't challenge them, they just ride out the day and hope nothing happens. If you want to be part of a high-performing team you have got to tell yourself every day is the day you are going to make the hardest fire of your career and remind everyone else on the company that success is a by-product of team effort.

As you prepare for the hardest fire you will ever make, the idea that no one else is coming should also be part of your mental preparation. Yes, there are other fire department and allied agency resources that are on the assignment but consider a few scenarios.

What happens when you get dispatched as a single unit to investigate an alarm and you find a working fire when you arrive? This has happened more than once in my career. Is there any chance that there could be a civilian still inside this fire that you thought was just alarm bells? Now, in those first critical minutes of this call, your company is there by itself, and your actions will shape the entire outcome for this incident. What happens when you are dispatched to a working fire and the second due company is already on a CPR job? The clock is ticking and your company now has to do the work of two.

The high-performing teams can stay nimble and rapidly adjust to the situation. The reason why is because they have sat around the kitchen table and "war gamed" these exact scenarios. High performing teams ask each other, "if this, then what"? Don't get carried away with this because if you get too far down the rabbit hole the exercise will lose its value. Spend some time developing your plan B and C because there will be a time when these alternatives are very important.

The companies that do the best in curveball situations see flexibility as a critical aspect to their identity. There is a lot we can pre-plan, but there are many factors we cannot. Whereas discipline is a hallmark of high-performing teams, rigid adherence to schedules and procedures is not. We do not have all the information when we make a run. As we arrive, we try our best to gain situational awareness, but there can always be a gap between what we know and what is really happening. I am a big advocate of a playbook-type system that the Leesburg, Florida, Fire Department has adopted. As much as I believe in playbooks, I also know that the mindset of rigid adherence to the playbook can set us up for a disaster. High-performing teams embrace flexibility and decentralized decision-making as fundamental elements of their mindset. Being able to handle curveballs is what will set your team apart from all the others.

One of the most important aspects of the mindset issue is the ability to play the long game. There has been much said and deep research done about the current societal need for instant gratification. It is the world we live in, and we must accept this as part of the world we live within. The real problem is that instant gratification does not support our efforts to build that high-performing team. Quality does not happen overnight.

One of the four basic Special Operations Forces (SOF) Truths is that "Competent Special Operations Forces cannot be created after emergencies occur." It takes time and effort to produce a high-performing team. We all love it when our favorite team wins the championship, but we forget about all the five seasons that lead up to the big game. If you are the boss, then you must remind your members that playing the long game is critical to success. If you are a team member who wants to reach the status of a high performer then you have to embrace the journey.

At some point, it is quite natural for some of our members to lose the long game mindset. The grind that leads to high performance is not easy. Top performers can also fall prey to the perfectionist mindset and get very frustrated when it doesn't happen right now. The strong teams rely on each other to maintain a balanced mindset. When you work on relationships as much as you work on tasks, you build that environment where you can tell someone, "Take a deep breath, buddy."

The mindset that we must be perfect right now actually is one of the things that pull teams apart. One of the most rewarding parts of being on a high-performing team is the journey it took to get to that point. It is important to size up everyone on your team, all the time, to make sure the mindset is focused on the long game.

The last and probably most important thing about mindset is you have to share your vision with the other members of your team. So many times, failure is a by-product of inaccurate or negative assumptions. Whatever parts of the mindset I have described you want to incorporate into your team, they don't belong to the team until you share them.

We all have a viewpoint that is exclusively our own. No matter how plainly you see an item, others might not share your view. When you start sharing your ideas with others, you are really building relationships, and this is one of the areas where high-performing teams set themselves apart from all the others.

As you walk down this path make sure you have a sound reason behind what you say. As you share you also open yourself up to questions. Your teammates might not see the importance of some of the elements of your mindset. Be ready to explain yourself, give good reasons why what you think is important and how the team can use this to improve. Stick to your guns if you feel very strongly about something but also remember that sometimes it's ok to compromise instead of building a conflict. Choose wisely the hills you are willing to die on.

Chapter Nuggets

- There are many different aspects to the mindset for high-performing teams.
- High-performing teams value the role that mindset plays.
- Working and leading with a servant's heart is common among high-performing teams.
- "Own" your response local as if your family lived there.
- Find a way to manage the negative feelings that come to everyone eventually.
- You will be the ones who respond to the hardest fire you will ever make. Does your mindset prepare you for this event?
- Not everyone is going to share the mindset you have, and it's ok to disagree.
- High performing teams understand that playing the long game is the only way to achieve greatness.

HIGH PERFORMING TEAMS

There are so many factors that go into building and maintaining a high performing team it is easy to get lost in the details. The little things always add up, and the more we pay attention to them, the higher the chance of having a high-performing team. It is critical to understand the converse of that statement; if we fail to pay attention to the little details, the chance of building a high-performing team is greatly decreased. Let's look at some of these realities.

The fundamental piece of building a high-performing team is to make sure your members understand the team dynamic. Firefighters are great at making assumptions. Does the new guy/girl know about working on a team, or do you just assume they know? That might have been somewhat accurate a few generations ago, but society has changed and that newly assigned member might be in the dark when it comes to functioning on a team.

Here is a simple test you can use when the new person walks through the door. Ask them if they have ever played team sports or if they have ever been in the military. If the answer is no, then you have to think they might not understand the team dynamic. These people could very well have spent their formative years not really engaged with a team. They might not understand the basic team concept of we win as a team, or we lose as a team. They might be just focused on their role without understanding everyone else's success depends on them doing their job. These folks might not understand that someone on the team is a little off; their job is to step in and pick up the slack.

In my mind, the most important element is that they are accountable to the team, and the team will give them both positive and negative feedback. Positive feedback is easy to take, but if you haven't gotten negative feedback from a peer, who can be a tough pill to swallow. To be successful, everyone on the team needs to know the basic requirements of being a team member. If they don't, then it is our job to teach them. Don't think you can hold someone accountable to a system they don't understand. So, seeing how I mentioned the dreaded word "accountability" in the last paragraph let's dive into the realities of accountability. Before you even think about holding someone accountable, have the standards been clearly explained? It is not uncommon to hear firefighters say their department really needs accountability. I have been brought into organizations because there was a lack of accountability. All I can say is watch out. Most times when you hear people asking for accountability, they are asking for something they don't really understand. To them, accountability is some nebulous concept that they have never really seen. When accountability walks through the door, everything gets real, really quick.

A lot of times, when firefighters say their organization needs accountability, they are really saying firefighter x or captain y needs to be held accountable. As soon as standards are set and actions start to happen, those people who championed accountability might become the loudest anti-accountability voices. They become concerned that they might be next because the people who spend their time measuring others normally don't spend enough time measuring themselves.

As I previously stated, for there to be accountability then there must be standards by which you judge when someone needs to be held accountable. I strongly believe in making these standards known from day one in the form of an expectations memo. Earlier in this book, I got into a deep dive about expectations memos, and I don't want to belabor the point. Let me just say, putting something in someone's hand really reinforces the importance of these expectations/standards. As important as it is to have these standards, you must also explain the "why" behind the memo. Some people might put a negative connotation on having standards like "if I don't do this then I am going to be in trouble." If that is the message you allow to be sent the effectiveness of your standards will decrease. The better track to take is to frame your conversations about standards from a positive perspective:

Welcome to the team. Our goal is for you to be successful in your role and enjoy your time with us. We want you to know what we expect, so here are our standards. We think for someone to be successful, they need to know what is expected of them and this is why our team has developed these standards/expectations. Take some time to review these. Let us know if you have any questions or if there are areas you think we can help you to strengthen your skills.

On high performing teams, accountability is not the sole function of the boss. Everyone on the team has a role in accountability, and there are many reasons for this. The boss might not be able to see something that needs to be addressed. The boss might be the one who is slipping, or they might be having a bad day as we all do sometimes. It should not matter who is the one that needs to be held accountable, and it really shouldn't matter who does the accounting. The team has set a standard that everyone knows. When there is a gap, action needs to be taken.

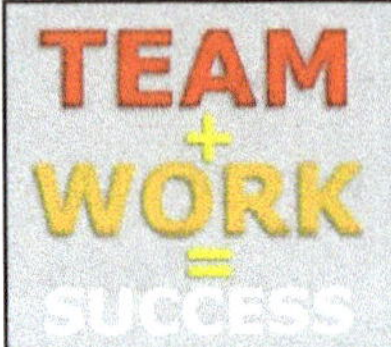

On high performing teams, accountability is not the sole function of the boss. Every team member has a role in accountability.

The good part is that if you have a high-performing team the member who is the one more than likely knows they are the one and they will step up before anyone has to say something. There is some real beauty when this happens, and it should be the goal we are working toward. As I have already said, to get here, you must play the long game, this type of behavior does not happen overnight.

Actions will always have consequences, some of them good and some of them not so good. High-performing teams know this, and they gear their actions toward the positive. There will always be choices that have to be made. The high performers know that they must make good decisions now, with consideration for what will come of their decisions. Just because this is what you want from your team, don't assume everyone thinks like this. I already talked about how some people might not have an understanding of the team environment, and likewise, not everyone fully appreciates the concept of actions and consequences.

As you begin to build your team, this is a conversation that needs to be had. Some might think this is just some of that "touchy feely" stuff but the details really matter. If you want your folks to think like this then talk to them about this. The strong teams do not leave things to chance, and they know if it can happen it probably will. Take some time to front-load this concept so you are not doing damage control after the fact.

The best teams with the best members will eventually end up in a less than desirable situation or have a less than desirable outcome. This is when you just roll with the punches. As simple as this sounds, I have found it to be at times a very hard thing to do. Human nature will work against you in these situations. People will become depressed, sometimes they will look to place blame, they will get frustrated, question their own abilities, or question the abilities of the leader to lead. No matter what combination of negatives begin to creep into the team's mindset, it must be addressed. If left unchecked, these negative reactions to a tough situation are like compounding interest. What starts out small grows exponentially and quickly.

One of the traits of high-performing teams is they hold resilience in high regard. They can endure tough situations and not let those situations affect their future performance. Think about quarterbacks like Tom Brady, Peyton Manning, or Mathew Stafford. Among their many attributes they have a reputation as being great comeback quarterbacks. Down late in the game, they just roll with the punches and find a way to lead their team to a victory. This same characteristic is vital for your team.

Every community has its 9/11 event coming. No matter the size or complexity of your response local something is going to happen that tests your resolve and capabilities. I spent over seven years as the Fire Chief in Sunrise Beach, Missouri and experienced some of the most difficult situations of my career. A member's suicide, multiple fatality fires, off-duty fatal accidents, and so on.

One of the most drastic incidents and one that shows the true importance of our resilience was an accident involving one of our apparatus. We experienced a rapid freezing on our roads and our Quint overturned when it hit a patch of ice. The rig ended up on its side in a ditch. The captain made an urgent transmission and our Squad Company, and I arrived shortly after the rig came to rest.

We were able to extricate the chauffeur and as they were transporting him to the hospital the Captain from the Squad asked me if I wanted them to start making the other runs that were in our District. With all that I was trying to manage I didn't realize there were several other incidents that needed attention. With the poor road conditions and the travel time for our mutual aid partners, the Squad Company was the closet resource.

Even though they had just dealt with a traumatic incident, seeing one of our rigs totaled and one of their co-workers injured, that company was able to get back on their rig and respond to help the citizens of our fire district. I must say this is one of the proudest days of my career and it demonstrates that resilience is an important attribute for your team no matter what the size of your community or your department.

The accident I described above was just one serious event our department experienced during the time I was there. We responded to several fatality fires, two of them involving multiple children. Our boat responded to a fatality boat accident during a major racing event, and our members were the ones who assisted in extricating the boat crew. One of our popular members left the department and shortly thereafter died by suicide. All these things happened in small town America to a small fire district. As hard as these events were on us, we still had a duty to protect and serve our community. We had to maintain our mission focus while making sure our people were OK. This is not an easy task, but the high performing teams understand that being able to roll with punches is one of the things that make them high performers. If you are not talking about this ability with your members do not expect this characteristic to magically appear when you need it.

To reinforce a point that I have already made several times, trust among the members is an absolute necessity. When a team is going through tough times trust is the glue that will hold them together and trust is built on having strong relationships in the team. We spend a lot of time maintaining tools and equipment but often come up short in maintaining our relationships with those we spend a third of our life within close quarters. Make a habit of doing something for the team every day. It doesn't have to be some monumental task. In fact, the small things often make the largest impression. Empty the trash can, answer the phone so others don't have to get up, ask how someone else's son or daughter did at a ball game. These little gestures will make deposits in the trust bank and that bank will be needed one day.

You are not going to like everyone you work with, but that does not mean you don't need to have some type of relationship with them. No matter what you think, there will come a time when you need that person to help you navigate the storms all fire companies face. Put your feelings aside and start to ask yourself some hard questions. What is it about that person you don't like? Sometimes the way we think doesn't really make sense and all we need to do is ask this question of ourselves for us to realize our impressions are not accurate. Have you approached this person about this thing you find annoying or unacceptable? If you are going to draw a conclusion then maybe you need to have the courage to bring this issue up.

Would it be possible that the person in question doesn't realize there is an issue? Be professional and be polite, but if you don't discuss the issue, it will show up at the worst possible time. Don't forget that you are human too.

Some of the things you do might bother people as much as the things they do that bother you. Building relationships is a two-way street. As much as you expect people to be open to what you have to say, they get a say too. You have to be willing to listen, take a deep breath, and separate your emotions from the conversation. High performing teams work on their relationships every day and they do not allow anything that gets in the way of building healthy relationships with each other.

The people you associate with have a strong influence on who you are. It has been said, " Show me your friends, and I will show you your future. In firefighter lingo, Chief Shannon Stone has said, "Hang around five stud firefighters, and you will become the sixth; hang around five sh!# heads, and you will become the sixth." Over the course of five decades, I have seen this repeatedly. You spend a lot of time with your team, but you spend a lot of time away from your team. The people you associate with on a regular basis have a strong influence on the person you are when you are with the team. Sometimes people will overlook the negative to be accepted by others. The popular person does not always support what you desire for your end state.

Sometimes people find it easier to go along than try to swim upstream against the loudest voice in the room. At some point you will have to make a hard decision for yourself. If you want to be part of excellence, you must shut out the noise that does not support excellence. On the surface, surrounding yourself with good people seems like a simple concept. Well, a lot of what sounds simple can be very difficult. How do you decide who the people you want in your circle are? How do you figure out the ones who will support your growth in being a good team member?

To identify the ones that I want in my circle, I have used a concept I call "The 5". I ask myself, who are the five firefighters I want with me in the most gnarly fire at which I will operate? I am in a dark, smoky, hot hallway, trying to make the push to the back bedroom, where there is a report of a child trapped. In this situation, who are the ones I know beyond any doubt I can trust to help me make that push? I have found that the people who make my list are not just good on the fireground, they are good people. They understand the value of being a good team member. They appreciate the importance of the mission. They are all in for the group and place little on the self-serving behaviors we see in some firefighters. When you have your list, start to think about why you named those firefighters to be the ones. When you spend some time thinking about this, a list of characteristics and traits will begin to appear.

Now you have a good idea of the characteristics and traits of the people you want in your circle. Get to know these people. High performers will generally want to be force multipliers. High performers understand that part of their purpose is to help others become high performers, and they will help you to join their ranks. Is there a skill that they do so well that made you add them to your list? Ask them how they got so good at that skill. Ask them if they have a tip that can help you be better on the fireground. Don't be a phony suck up, but a simple compliment like "hey I noticed how you did ______ and I really think that was pretty slick."

Sometimes we forget that high performers are just regular human beings that happen to be good at something. All human beings like a little praise, and a simple complement can be the first step in building a strong (here it comes again) relationship.

Not only will this technique help you identify people you want in your circle, but it will also give you a list of traits that you can strive for in your own firefighting game. One reality of high-performing teams is that the team members are constantly looking to improve themselves. They are not happy with the status quo; they are always looking for a competitive edge. They seek to improve the team by working on themselves. They help those around them to be better, realizing that as we all improve the performance of the team will improve. The strongest team is made up of people who are not afraid to be self-reflective. People who spend a little quiet time every day asking difficult questions of themselves are the type of people who can be counted on when the going gets tough.

It is very easy to think that "The 5" is just comparing yourself to others, and this is a false assumption. "The 5" gives us a list of attributes that we can work to improve. I am not any of the people on my 5. I use this concept to develop the skills I have identified as beneficial to the best that I can. Do not use this technique to be someone else, use this to be better today than you were yesterday and better tomorrow than you are today.

There is one other use for "The 5" concept. Once you have done your thinking and identified the traits that these folks exhibit that put them on your list, you now have a list you can share with others. It is totally unrealistic to think that everyone on your team is going to think the same way.

Maybe you can throw some of your thoughts out to the group and see how they respond? Try this one night at the kitchen table when the company is eating dinner, say, "Hey. I've been thinking that some of the top characteristics for being a good firefighter are x, y, and z. What do you all think?" You might be surprised that the other team members think the same way you do, and if that is the case, then great. You are headed in the right direction. Maybe they come up with items you didn't think about.

Your list isn't the perfect list; it's just your list. Maybe something someone else says gets you thinking and you add that characteristic to your list. You have now given one of your team members the chance to help you get better. I call that a win/win.

From the 30,000-foot view, your statement might move the team from having a simple dinner conversation into a deep discussion of what we want our team to be and what we value. High-performing teams are not afraid to engage in these types of conversations. Don't expect everyone else to do the heavy lifting for excellence; you are as much a part of the team as anyone else, and you need to contribute to the process.

Chapter Nuggets

- Not everyone understands the dynamics of working on a team and if a newly assigned member doesn't, it's our responsibility to teach them.
- Everyone on the team is accountable and we are not afraid to hold each other accountable.
- For accountability to work the team must have clear standards to judge performance and those standards must be known by all the team members.
- We understand that actions have consequences.
- Not everything is going to be perfect, and we can roll with the punches.
- We surround ourselves with good people and we eliminate the people who do not support our vision of excellence.

THE FINER POINTS

Building a high-performing team is an ongoing process. You can have a lot of success, have great team members, your reputation is stellar, and all seems right with the world. Congratulations, you have done great work but, be careful. Many high performing teams have failed at this point. They feel like they have arrived. They took their foot off the gas. They started to say to themselves, "Man, we really are good." These attitudes are the start of the slow downward slide to complacency. Before you know it, someone is saying it's good enough. Now the train is really starting to fall off the tracks. If you want to achieve and maintain your standards of high performance, then you must do the work every day and pay attention to the finer points.

I think this is a good spot to spend some time talking about complacency. Complacency is the poison for high-performing teams. The two just cannot co-exist. If we want to maintain our status as a high-performing team, then we must know how complacency happens and how to avoid falling into the trap.

The first thing to think about is that complacency implies at one time there was some measure of awareness and skills. You do not see recruits at the academy being complacent. Where you actually see this happening is in firehouses with experienced crews. This tells me that complacency can happen to anyone, and that fact alone is very helpful in avoiding the spiral into poor performance. If we know it, we can prepare for it, and this allows us to prevent it from ever happening.

Complacency does not happen overnight. The transition from high performing to complacent is a slow developing process. You look at yourself every day in the mirror and probably don't notice any significant difference in your appearance. Go get a picture of yourself from about 5 years ago and look at the difference. Kind of eye-opening, isn't it? This is exactly how complacency happens.

Chief Scott Thompson often mentions the "slow drift to failure." Complacency often happens at a rate so slow, you don't realize it is happening. The moment you realize you have drifted to complacent is often when there is a critical mission failure on the fireground or a significant issue at the firehouse. Avoiding complacency requires a constant effort to ensure it does not find its way into your team.

The last thing I will mention about complacency is that someone along the way let it happen. Someone stopped pushing the member to be a little bit better, to work hard every day in the firehouse, to keep their focus on high performance.

This is a perfect example of a lack of accountability and the normalization of deviance. Someone on the team didn't step up and speak out. At some point the team allowed itself to deviate from their stated norms. The company made a run for an automatic fire alarm and didn't wear all their gear. They get away with it once, and now the next time they get that same run when it is hot outside, and they are tired, they fall back on the last time when the run turned out to be just a faulty system. Hence begins the slow drift to failure and the slow downhill slide to complacency. What I have just described is how every complacent firefighter and team ends up being that way.

Knowing how complacency sneaks into our daily routine is a powerful tool you can use to avoid complacency and is a characteristic of a high-performing team. If we know the process, we can share this information with everyone on the team. We can tell all the team members to watch for it and empower them to say something when appropriate. I have already talked about accountability and the importance of everyone being able to speak up. Fighting complacency is why the freedom to speak up is so important. Don't be misled into thinking this is only the boss's job. Everyone has a role to play in fighting complacency, and the high-performing teams rely on everyone to help uphold the standard.

High-performing teams are the ones that pursue excellence, and you have to widen your exposure if excellence is what you desire. Look at any successful sports team. There are many venues available to firefighters nowadays to enhance their operational abilities. If you are content to live exclusively within the walls of your firehouse, then at some point your team will become stagnant.

In today's world, if you are standing still, then you are actually moving backwards. Failing to widen your scope will eventually encase your team in a silo, which in turn becomes an echo chamber. Now we set ourselves up for the downhill slide to lackluster performance. Look past the walls of your firehouse and this adverse course of action will not happen.

As you widen your scope, you must remember several of the points I have already made. You must be open to new ideas. Be cautious as you investigate a new tactic or technology. Just because it is new does not mean it will be a good fit. This new thing might be coming from a person or department that is completely different from yours. Their response district, staffing, and apparatus can all impact what they are doing and can be completely different from your operational environment. Whatever you research must work at your fires, not someone else's.

You must concentrate on the message, not the messenger. In high-performing teams, there will always be an element of ego. High-performing teams did not get that way because they are made up of easy-going, laid-back surfer-type people. For us to benefit from what is out there, we must be willing to listen to all our members.

I have already mentioned the importance of giving everyone on your team the chance to be heard. You must also be willing to listen to what is being said. That one person you just don't particularly like, who is the most junior member of the team, might have a suggestion that you never thought about. We want to leverage the collective wisdom of all our members and sometimes some of our members bring something to the table from an outside source.

Do not rush to judgment just because of who brought the idea to the table.

Social media and the internet have added more to the fire service, both good and bad, than almost anything I can remember. In days gone by you would have to travel to widen your scope. I appreciate the fact that this costs time and money, things that can be in short supply for those raising children, paying mortgages, and just trying to make ends meet. You must remember there are always two sides to the coin. For as much good content as there is on social media, there is a lot of junk out there too.

Do not rush to judgment just because of who brought the idea to the table.

Anyone can start up a Facebook page and say just about anything they want. There are some very good sources out there, but you must take everything with a grain of salt. Some people just want the recognition that goes along with having a social media site and are more interested in collecting a huge number of followers than they are concerned with sharing quality information. As you digest the latest Facebook or internet fad, pump the brakes a little. Look at the source. Does the person have the background and experience to be championing what they post? Does the idea or concept make sense? First impressions might be positive, but when you stop and think about it just doesn't hold up. The most important thing to remember is, try this new way on the drill ground before you do it on the fireground. Someone's emergency should not be your experiment.

I cannot leave the conversation about social media without sharing some of my experiences and thoughts on how we can make the platform a positive place to exchange information. I have always said that my way of doing things is just a way. I have never thought my way is the best way or the only way, it is just a way that happens to work for me with my skills, my equipment, and in my operational environment.

I also encourage healthy disagreements. I made a post about carrying a box light, and a highly respected firefighter disagreed with my concept. He even called me, and we had a great twenty-minute discussion. I must say he made a lot of great points that I included in a follow-up post. Conversations like this are productive and make us all better.

I made another post about carrying portable radios and included the link in my post to the Fairfax County study. I got a lot of grief from that one. One person just ripped everything I said apart. He said he had an extensive communications background from the US military and I didn't know what I was talking about. When I responded by asking if he had read the study that was linked to the story and was the basis for my suggestions, he danced around without answering the question.

When I went back to his FB page his tag line was "I am a very intelligent person, and I don't give a F__K what anyone else says." The conversation ended with a delete and block.

After a while another person said that the study was wrong about the possibility of the radio falling out of the pocket. They said they had been using their turnout coat radio pocket for twenty years and had never had their radio fall out of the pocket. They said if the study was correct, then their radio should have been lost a long time ago. Ok, so if you have been driving a car for twenty years and have never had an accident, then you shouldn't have to worry about using a seat belt? I only share these stories to underscore the need to vet the information you see on social media.

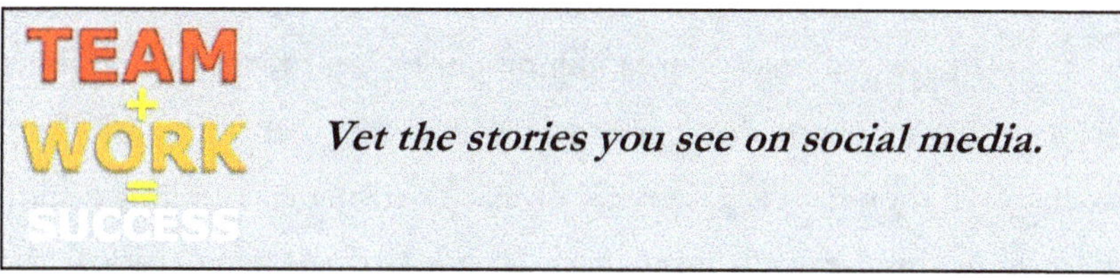

YouTube is another example of a great source of information that can also be a train wreck. Much of what I said about social media applies to what you can see on YouTube. Dig into the back story a little. What is the background of the people making the video? Does what they are demonstrating make sense and does it apply to your operational environment?

Remember that the instructional videos are staged. I do this with my videos. I make sure the camera angles are correct, the lighting is optimal and the dialogue comes out correctly. Just because you see it on YouTube does not mean it will have an application for your team. If you see something that looks good, do some training. Make sure what looks good on the TV at the firehouse brings an increased capability on the fireground. This applies to what you see on my YouTube channel and social media pages. No one has all the answers, and no one has the best way for you to operate.

A high-performing team will take care of each other. Excellence will always attract critics. There is no escaping this, some of the critics are up front and in your face. These are probably the easiest to deal with because you know right where they stand. Other critics are more devious. They might smile to your face all the while they are sharpening the knife to stick in your back when you turn around. Regardless of the type of critic, members of high performing teams do not allow their fellow members to be put down. You must stand up and push back in these situations.

When you hear people talking about your team or members on your team, say you don't appreciate their comments and ask them to stop. If they don't, just walk away. You made your point, and there is nothing else to be gained. In a lot of these situations, the people doing the talking are just bullies. They do what they do because no one stands up to them. As soon as someone does push back their courage often turns out to be the size of a pea.

It can be very hard to walk away from someone who is bad-mouthing your team or a member, but you must be able to disconnect. Sometimes these people are bullies and will just back down. Unfortunately, sometimes these folks are just looking for a fight. Either way, people who talk badly about others normally don't bring a lot to the table. They are so focused on everyone else; they don't have the time and energy needed to be good themselves. They want to prove they are the smartest people in the room. They will twist the truth to fit their agenda and will do everything they can to bring you down to their level.

High-performing teams do not sink to the level of poor performers. At times like this, I remember this quote from Mark Twain: "Never argue with stupid people, they will drag you down to their level and then beat you with experience."

When you don't allow people to badmouth a team member, you send a very important message. You are saying that if you mess with any of us then you are messing with all of us. I am not telling you to keep boxing gloves inside your locker or challenging people to meet you in the parking lot. You are letting everyone know you belong to a solid team. You are telling the other people on your team that you have their back and they can trust you.

As I have said before, trust is an absolute for the development of a high-performing team, and your willingness to defend the other members of the team goes a long way in building this trust. Firehouse drama has a way of sucking the life out of everything. If you leave the door just slightly cracked the negative energy will find its way into your team. I have found that pushing back on the critics is an important part of defending your workspace. If you do not allow others to talk badly about your team or any of your members, the critics are likely to go find other targets.

Just like bullies, most of the critics look for the low-hanging fruit. If they can't get a response from you, then there is a good chance they will move to another target. If nothing else, they will probably just talk behind your back, and if that is their game, who cares? At this point you have shut the door on them having any influence on your workplace. This is not an easy thing to do but over the course of time you will come to see that the critics have little impact on you, your team, and the team's performance.

The reality of being a firefighter is that our workplace is full of danger. I don't mean to overstate this, and I do not let this fact deter me from prosecuting our mission. If we put too much emphasis on safety, then we will hamper our abilities to operate in a manner that saves lives and protects property. When I think about the risks on the fireground, I often remind myself that the definition of safety is a condition that exists without risk. You cannot make a run without exposing yourself to some type of risk.

High-performing teams understand the true nature of our business and work to manage the risk. Everything up to this point has an impact on managing risk. You can't just choose the easy stuff. You must address the difficult issues like standards, accountability, and tough relevant training to provide your members with the ability to manage risk on the fireground.

Even when we do everything right, bad things can still happen. What sets the high-performing teams apart is the common knowledge among all the members that if something goes sideways, the rest of the team is coming for you. Knowing this simple fact can help manage the natural fear that people will have when you put them in dangerous situations and allow them to concentrate on the mission.

It does not matter how many years you have been on the job or how many fires you have gone to. You are still a human being, and you still have the natural survival instinct. There is no way you can train this facet out of someone and to be honest you really don't want your team members to lose this element of their personality.

When one suppresses this to the point where they don't feel fear, they become reckless. Reckless people are a hindrance to performance and should be avoided at all costs. If you really want to have a high-performing team, then you must have this conversation with your team members. It is a great starting point for new members and an issue that should occasionally come up in your ongoing training.

Knowing that the team will do what it takes to get a member out of a tight spot not only builds trust among the members, but it also allows people to focus on the mission at hand. As much as a reckless firefighter will cause problems, a timid member will not allow you to win the fight. Risk management is all about finding the edge of the envelope and being comfortable operating there for as long as it takes to shape the outcome of the incident. The fight is won when our team generates its operational tempo faster than the fire. Knowing that every member of the team is present in their position, capable in their abilities, and will live by the mantra that no one will be left behind is what allows the team to function at a high level in dangerous situations. There are no two ways about this. If you want to have a high-performing team, everyone must be able to say, "I was scared, but I knew you would come for me."

Chapter Nuggets

- To build a high-performing team, you must expand your scope beyond your firehouse.
- High-performing teams have a strong sense of togetherness and will support each other when critics want to take cheap shots.
- The fireground is a dangerous place and for a team to perform at a high level the members need to have faith that no matter what, the other members will come for them.

RELATIONSHIPS

As I have been working on this book, I have been very fortunate to get feedback from outstanding fire service leaders and human beings. One of my dear friends called me after reading through the first eleven chapters and said there was a lot of great info but, I need one more chapter. I was a little confused at first. I thought I had covered all the bases, so I asked what that chapter should be. In a one-word reply, he said, "relationships."

I had thought that was a theme I had woven into all the chapters, but then I started thinking. Relationships are really the bottom line. When you peel the onion all the way back, solid relationships are the foundation of high-performing teams. Without these relationships, the team will never be able to reach its potential.

So, let's take a deep dive into relationships.

To build a solid relationship, you really need to know your true north, what you will stand for, and what you will not compromise. Some people will go along to get along. They are easily swayed by popular opinion. They really don't like to make waves, and they will avoid confrontation at all costs. These characteristics will not put you in good light with a high-performing team.

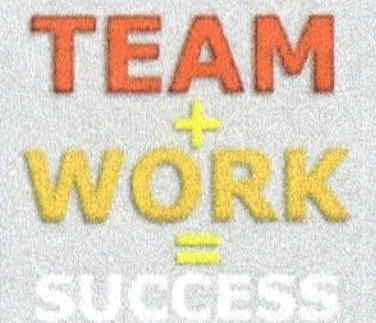

Solid relationships are the foundation of high-performing teams.

If you have never watched the Nick Saban video on YouTube where he discusses high performers and mediocre people, you should. The coach lays this concept out in easy-to-understand terms, and his record of success says to me he knows what he is talking about. Firefighters are very smart people. If you are putting on an act they can see right through you.

To illustrate this point, ask yourself a few simple questions. The first question is why are you in the fire service? Are you here to be a servant? Do you understand the nature of our calling and what is expected of us? The second question is, what do you do every day when no one is watching, to support how you answered the first question? The last question is what are your non-recoverables, the things that someone would do from which they cannot recover? If you have to spend a lot of time thinking about these questions or if you have a long rambling answer, then you probably need to spend a little time refining your answers.

I don't mean to come off as some righteous know-it-all; I am just saying that the members of high-performing teams have asked themselves these questions, and they can answer them without hesitation in a few short sentences. If you want to be one of them, then you need to have your answers ready to go.

As part of laying your relationship foundation you must look at yourself in the mirror and ask, am I a good person? There are a lot of shaky people in the world who have a clearly defined true north for themselves. They know exactly what they want and are not afraid to do whatever it takes to get there. The problem is you couldn't trust them as far as you could throw them with one hand tied behind your back.

Think about some of the sports teams that were loaded with talent and couldn't make the playoffs. More times than not a contributing cause of the team coming up short was locker room cancer. A very talented person who really didn't care about the team.

I have seen this in every rank. You cannot produce excellence with bad people. Let's go back to question-and-answer time. Could the people on your time trust you to watch their kids? Would the people on your team have any hesitation loaning you their car? Could the people on your team trust you with a secret (one that did not have any negative consequences)? These might seem like little things, but they truly matter. If you want to be accepted by good people and remember that high-performing teams are made up of good people, you must be a good person.

When we talk about relationships, one of the things that is important is the life span of the relationship. Most teams will at some point have a translation. People are promoted, some people transfer to a new assignment, some people might take a temporary detail to say the training division, maybe some will retire. A healthy relationship is one that will stand the test of time. Not every member of the teams you will be on during your career will turn into lifelong companions, but if you go about doing the right thing the right way, some will. These are the people who will always be there for you.

This job can put some hard miles on a person and having people you can reach out to will help ease that burden. If you don't have a few of these people in your corner, you will carry all the weight by yourself.

There are two big problems with this. The first is carrying all the weight alone is just not healthy. I can't help but think that with all the issues we have in the fire service with mental health, a lack of trusted relationships among members is a contributing factor.

The second thing to think about is if you can share some of the burdens this job produces with a trusted confidant or two you will eat up a lot of your mental bandwidth ruminating about the issue. This is bandwidth that will not be available at the apartment fire with people trapped. To be at your best when it is needed the most you have to be able to think clearly.

The concept of relationships goes beyond your current team. Relationships are force multipliers. The positive attributes you build in your current assignment will carry forward to your next assignment. Strong teams build other strong teams. Not only will you carry forward what you learned in your time, but the positive influence you had on other people will continue to live in their new assignments. Often, we look at today and tomorrow, but that is a short-sighted approach.

The work we do to build healthy relationships is not a finite goal that we reach and then move on. I liken relationship building to what happens when you drop a rock into a body of water. The ripples this action causes spread from the initial point of contact in far-reaching circles. What you do today will be felt in the future so why not make sure it will be a positive influence?

Those who really care look past their tenure and concern themselves with the future of the team. There is no way you can have a positive impact on the future if you do not have good relationships in the present. I am sure you have heard some of the "old heads" talking about the younger generation. A lot of times these conversations are anything but positive.

When we allow this to happen, we limit the possibility of the transfer of knowledge and wisdom. The "old heads" are the ones who have been in position the longest. They have made the runs, they are familiar with the intricacies of the response local, and they have seen things the junior members have not.

When we don't have good relationships among our present team members, the transfer of critical information will stop when these folks walk out the door for the last time. This book is what I will call a 50/50 process. Half of what I have written are my impressions and observations spanning fifty years. The other half are things that senior people shared with me. If it weren't for those people wanting to build a relationship of trust and respect, that transfer of knowledge would never have happened.

You have a role in building the legacy of your team. The team will continue after you are gone. The picture below was taken at the graduation ceremony for the 1st recruit academy our department ever held. Out of that one class came the recently retired fire chief of the Cherry Hill Fire Departemt as well as the current chief of the department.

I was the officer in charge of the academy and spent every day with the members of the class. My involvement with the class was considerable. I am not claiming my influence on these men was the reason for their success. They earned their position through dedication and hard work. My hope is that I was able to share some knowledge and insights that helped them grow into their leadership positions.

I have always worked to develop high-performing teams, and one of the fundamental aspects of my approach was the concern for the team after I left. What was I doing today that would add value tomorrow? Could I offer something; knowledge, skills or abilities that would let the team continue toward excellence after I was gone? Could I be a resource that could offer an unbiased opinion? I would like to say that I can answer yes to all these questions. I accepted the detail to the recruit academy not because of the status it gave me in the organization, I went to the academy to help build a strong foundation for the fire department.

Building relationships isn't just about what you will receive as a by-product or the future of your organization, it is being in the position to help others. High performing teams often describe themselves as family, and the fire service is all about the brotherhood/sisterhood. If we believe in this and want it to be more than just a catch phrase, we must put our words into action. There will be times when someone needs help, an encouraging word, or just a chance to vent and let off some steam.

One of the most important things you can do as a member of a high performing team is to be there when these times happen. Never take for granted the value in relationships, they are the foundation for excellence.

What you do will always come back to you. When I was leading the Academy, I never thought about what I would get out of the program. I just wanted to help steer a generation of firefighters who would be part of the job long after I left in the right direction. Years later, they gave me a gift that I will never forget.

The next picture was taken on my last shift at the Cherry Hill Fire Department. The Chief and I had always been runners. That morning, before my tour started, we met for an early morning run. As we made the last turn back to the firehouse the members from the first recruit academy class joined in on the run. They were all wearing tee shirts with my caricature printed on it and a banner commemorating "Reilly's Final Run." I hadn't worked with some of these people for years, but they all came out on an early Saturday morning to give me a gift I will never forget.

Chapter Nuggets

- High-performing teams understand the importance of building strong relationships among their members.
- Good people are the ones who build quality relationships.
- Understand your "why" and develop your own sense of true north.
- Relationships should be as much about what you can offer others as what you get out of the relationships.
- The value of your relationships can last long after you leave the team. Appreciate your part of the legacy in your organization.

BULLETS FOR THE BOSSES

High-performing teams are led by great bosses. My time in the fire service has shown me again the true importance of the officer. I do not mean to diminish the role of the firefighter, and I have seen some excellent firefighters overcome poor leaders. At some point, the effectiveness of the team will suffer if the boss isn't performing up to the highest standards. To help the current bosses and those who aspire to be in a leadership position, here are some of the things that I feel are critical for high-performing bosses.

No One Made You Take the Promotion, So Do Your Job

I have gone to many promotion ceremonies, and I have never seen someone hold a gun to the head of the person being promoted. You chose to take the promotion; no one forced you. As a chief, I would offer a promotion and make the member say "Yes, I want to be promoted."

This becomes a verbal contract between us. My role was to support the newly promoted officer, offer guidance, help them mature into their role, but in turn they needed to do their job.

They had to set expectations, hold people accountable, have difficult conversations, fix problems, and take responsibility for the members under their command. When a chief calls you about performance or an issue they aren't wanting to hear about how firefighter X made a mistake or did something wrong. They are asking why you let that happen. Command comes with a heavy burden, so be prepared to accept the good with the bad.

If Your Team Does It, You Own It

You are the bottom line for your team. You must take ownership of everything the team does or does not do. I have always told my officers they have the ultimate responsibility for the firehouse and the fireground. When something does not go the way it should, the only person I want to speak with is the boss. This is the reality of being in charge. You will not endear yourself to your boss when your response to the difficult question involves throwing one of your members under the bus.

When officers do this, my impression is they are not fit to lead. Not all officers get this, but it is an important aspect of true leadership. You must also realize that a great way to kill the trust between you and your members is passing the blame on to them for something you allowed to happen.

Praise in Public and Discipline in Private is so True

No matter how "seasoned" a member might be, they are still a human being, and human beings will react in a favorable manner to positive comments. Don't go overboard and don't be overly dramatic. A simple "nice job" in front of everyone goes a long way.

If you have a high performing team at some point your boss is probably going to recognize you. When they do, put your success right back on the team. You might be the one who is building the culture, but the team is the one who is executing. Good bosses understand this and they will give credit to the ones below. If you are in this for recognition, then at some point you will fail as a boss.

If you want to lose your team, discipline somebody in front of the other members. This action shows you really don't respect your people. This is not to say that sometimes due to the nature of the situation you might have to take immediate action. Actions that endanger a member or members, any type of threatening behaviors or actions, and criminal actions are examples of when you must step up right away.

Don't Put Yourself in the Position I Can't Defend You

Just because you will be held accountable by your boss doesn't mean that your people will not have consequences if they do something stupid. Honest mistakes will be made, and people should not be afraid to make an honest mistake.

The only people who don't make mistakes are people who don't do anything. These are not the people we want on our teams. What I want my people to understand is I am always going to ask the question "At the time you did_____ what made you think this was the right decision."

Often, we don't see everything that is involved, we don't have all the facts or a clear picture. I want to have a full understanding before you make your decision. Once you have all the facts and the facts clearly point to a bad decision on their part, you must hold them accountable. The upside to this is if you have done all things that I have discussed in this book, it will be very rare when you must hold people accountable.

There is an Ebb and Flow to Being in Charge

Enjoy the good times because eventually, something will happen that will spill your apple cart. This is just the way it is, and it is totally unreasonable to think that you and your team will be immune to the realities of life. One of the critical traits of a good leader is how they react when things don't go well.

Your team will follow your lead and if you let your emotions get the best of you, you will see that reflected in your members. The worst thing is that sometimes the situation will not be fair. It's Ok to say you are not happy about a given situation, you just must maintain a level head and keep your team focused on the mission. Exactly how you will do this takes some time to figure out.

Sometimes you might let your people have a free fire zone for twenty minutes. Let them have their say, but at the end of the time stop the talk and move on. Remember though you are the leader and you just have to bite your tongue. If you get down in the trenches it will be very hard to stop the talk and get back to business. Your job is to be the leader and that means being the adult in the room.

Leaders Go First and Eat Last

Anytime you can go first at anything, do it! Leaders lead from the front. When your team is doing training evolutions, be the first one to do the evolution. You don't have to be perfect, in fact having some trouble shows your folks you are just like them, a human. If you don't have the courage to be first on the drill ground your people will start to wonder if you have the courage to lead them on the fireground.

There is a story about General Gavin of the 82nd Airborne Division during World War II. When asked where the General was, a soldier replied, "You will not find him back here, he is up at the front." This type of leadership means a lot to the people who you might very well out in harm's way.

Often in the firehouse there will be an occasion when a meal is served. No matter if it is just the evening meal or some type of occasion like a promotion or a retirement, leaders should always eat last. This is a symbolic gesture that tells your people they are important. This lets people know you are a servant leader.

People of a lesser rank might defer to you but graciously insist they go first. The small gesture sends a big message.

If You See It Coming, Stop It Before It Happens

Often, when my officers are dealing with an issue, they make a comment along the lines of, "Wow! I kind of saw this one coming." Well, if you saw it why didn't you stop it? This goes back to the very first point I made about doing your job. As a boss it is your job to have the difficult conversations and you need to have these conversations at the onset, not after the issue becomes an issue.

Most big problems start out as small problems. They only grow in size because someone didn't have the difficult conversation at the beginning. The conversation might be uncomfortable, but you stand a better chance for an easy fix if you act when the problem is just starting out.

Many times, especially with new officers, people will think that they are going to hurt the team dynamic if they have a difficult conversation. In reality you are doing more damage by not addressing the issue.

Everyone on the team sees what is happening and true professionals expect the leader to hold people accountable to the standards of the team. If you don't then you are hurting your moral responsibility as a leader and this will impact on how the team views you.

The other problem is now there is an issue that brings scrutiny about the team from the boss's boss. This will have a negative impact on the whole team. Manage your people in a way that upholds the standards and culture of your high performing team.

There is Always A Link Higher in the Chain Than You

We all have a boss but sometimes when you are a boss this is easy to forget. The way you interact with your boss impacts on your team in several ways. At some point you will need either support or resources from your boss. If you do not cultivate a healthy relationship with your boss, you might not get the support you need.

Let's say there is one slot to send a department member to outside training. One of your folks wants to go and there is an equally qualified member from another team that also wants to go. You have a less than productive relationship with your boss. The boss of the other member who wants to go to training has a healthy relationship with your common boss. Guess who is going to get the nod for the training.

The other thing to consider is how you interact with your boss sends a signal to your people to see how they can interact with you. If you want respect, then you must give respect. Some of your bosses are going to be great. Some of your bosses might be incompetent, micromanagers, or worse just bad human beings.

A good way to manage your boss' relationships is to treat your boss exactly how you want your people to treat you.

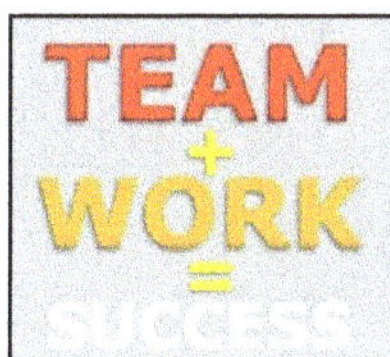

If you want respect, you give respect.

There are More of Them Than There are of You

You will always be outnumbered in the workplace. Your team sees everything you do or don't do. They hear everything you say or don't say. You are the boss and that is always the reality of your situation. Your message must be consistent with everyone.

They talk when you are not in the room so make sure you are not sending conflicting messages. Every new officer has had the experience of walking into a room and the conversation stops. This is a natural thing that catches some people off guard. The worst thing you can do is try to fit in so the team will include you in all the conversations. This will normally lead to trouble. You will relax your standards in order to be accepted. You will let little things go, and when you do these things will find a way to grow into big deals.

High performing teams need to have a boss and that is you. Understand there are times when the conversation stops and you just have to be comfortable with that.

When They Laugh at You, Laugh with Them

I must admit that I am the classic example of occasionally doing dumb stuff, but, hey, aren't we all? Having thin skin is one of the worst things you can have when you are a boss. I remember one time walking into a fire house when two of the members were holding court, doing a little skit that was making fun of me. Their backs were turned so that went on for a good minute before one of them got a feeling and said, "He's standing right behind us, isn't he?"

It would have been easy to pull out the disciplinary policy and made these guys extremely uncomfortable. Instead, I remembered the old adage that imitation is the sincerest form of flattery. In the performance of my duties, I might issue an order that could result in these guys getting killed. Our calling can be very serious at times, but it isn't serious all the time. If, as the boss, I am not willing to be the subject of some good-natured humor, then I have given up the right to lead these guys on the fireground. To this day whenever we get together we all have a good laugh about this. Isn't that really what being part of a team is about?

You Need to Know When to Get Up and Leave the Room

Don't get me wrong, I am not saying you should turn a blind eye to unacceptable behaviors. Boys will be boys is not an excuse to allow things to go in a way that is not acceptable to the standards you have set. You also need to realize that the company does not need to have the boss present for every conversation. If you have a strong team culture, then sometimes the members must have enough space and freedom to unwind a little. This is not going to happen if you are always present. Bosses should have a set time when they head to the office. You also need to be able to read the room. When you feel like it is time to leave, you are probably right. Think back to when you were a firefighter and I am sure you will remember times when you wished your boss had got up from the table. Don't overstay your welcome.

Everyone Wants You to Have The Difficult Conversations

Even in the best teams sometimes things need to be addressed. This is where you really earn your pay as the boss. These conversations are never fun, and it is easy to find a dozen excuses to not have the conversation. It is an isolated event, he/she is really a good person, everyone makes a mistake, and so on. Small missteps can really hurt a high performing team. In the firehouse environment everyone sees everything.

Not having this conversation can erode the faith your team members have in you. You are expected to be the gate keeper for the standards of your team and that means you have to have the difficult conversations when they are needed.

You Do Not Have to Attend Every Argument You are Invited To

Being the boss can put you in some difficult positions. No matter what type of culture you have built for your team, what expectations you have set, and how you run your firehouse day to day, remember that you are probably leading some hard charging Type A personalities. High performers can often have strong opinions, and this can lead to disagreements.

Provide a safe place for your team to express themselves.

It is very easy when this happens to feel as if you are being challenged or take this personally. Try your best not to do this. Let your people have a safe space to express themselves. Don't feel like you have to answer every question and defend every decision immediately. Sometimes it is best to say, "let me think about this." Sometimes your people are just looking to vent. Sometimes they have legitimate concerns. Whatever the case, take a quick read on the situation. If the conversation is emotionally charged, let the cake cool off a little. Whatever the case, think about the impact your actions will have after the conversation ends. Winning an argument can lose you the war.

Second Chances Should Have a Short Leash

Nobody is perfect and everyone deserves a second chance. I truly believe this and have given many people a second chance. Unfortunately, more time than not the second chance only belayed the final outcome. Patterns of behavior are very hard to break. When someone puts themselves in a bad position they need to make some immediate changes. The fire service does not have a lot of room for less-than-optimal performance. Don't be surprised when the person you had to correct repeats the same behavior. If you want to kill the morale on your team, let someone operate outside the expected norms. You would hope that the standards you have set and the reputation of your team would preclude the sub-standard performers from even walking in the door.

Sometimes you don't get a choice on who gets assigned to your team. Be prepared for when that person shows up, give them a second chance but with a short leash, and do not allow them to rear down what the team has worked so hard to build.

Some Lessons Will Come with a Huge Dose of Humility

Being a boss is not easy. No one was born with the skill set to be successful in this position and you will not get all the skills needed with your new badge. You must accept the fact that there is a huge learning curve in your new role. There is also a serious dichotomy in that you have much to learn but your boss expects you to be competent in your position. This will often lead you to make mistakes that are painful to experience. You must remember this dichotomy is part of the maturing process for new bosses.

As a very new, inexperienced incident commander I released the companies and left a fire scene when I thought everything was out. Fast forward two hours and the department gets a re-kindle for a working fire. I will say this is the first and last time that it ever happened. I did not personally walk through the fire building to make sure everything was out. A pile of clothes was smoldering in the closet which caused the rekindle.

There were several important lessons I learned from this. It would have been easy to blame the crew who reported everything was good, but I was the IC and the buck stopped with me. I could have walked through the structure to see for myself, but I didn't. I was content with taking someone's word for a critical decision that belonged to me. I could have left a company on the fire ground, but it was getting close to lunch and everyone wanted to get back to their stations. I choose to make everyone happy at the expense of leaving a fire watch at the scene.

These were hard lessons to learn, and I must admit they were very humiliating for me. It took me a lot of work to rebuild the trust my organization had in me after this fire. I am thankful that I was working for an organization that did believe in second chances, but I can tell you the leash was short.

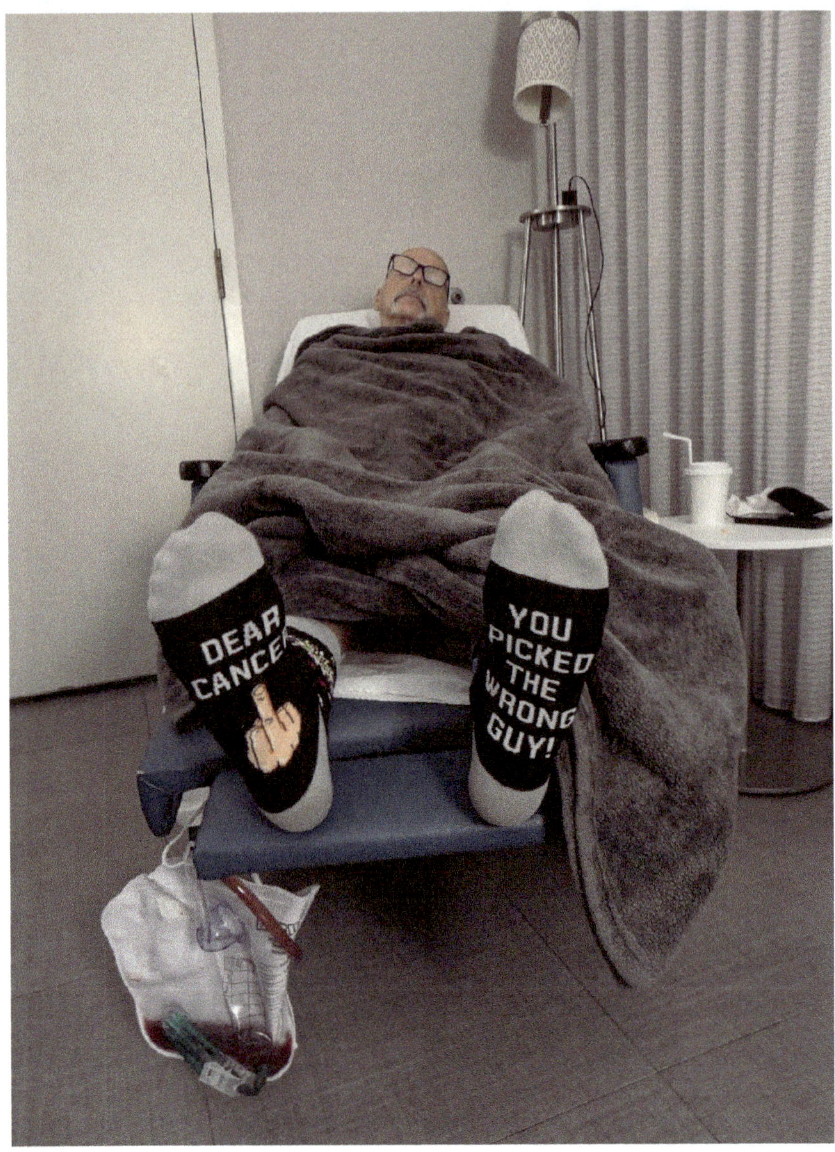
DEAR CANCER
YOU PICKED THE WRONG GUY!

EPILOGUE

As I was working on this book I got the news that no one really wants to hear, you have stage II prostate cancer. My diagnosis took about two months to be confirmed. I went through a series of tests and exams to determine what was happening. At each turn I was told, "this probably will not amount to anything, but let's just be on the safe side." These statements were made to help me process what was happening but in the back of my mind I had a strong suspicion that the final diagnosis would be cancer. I was right. I wish I weren't, but it does not work that way. I learned several things through this episode and here are some of the points that I want to share and that helped me through this difficult time.

The most important thing is you must be your own advocate. You must do your own research, decide for yourself what the best course of treatment is for you and your lifestyle. I was faced with several options, some of them good and some of them not so good. Each option came with side effects. After giving everything careful consideration my best choice became obvious. I chose to have the robot assisted radical prostatectomy and I have had a lot of success with this choice.

Being your own advocate is important, but having a care team makes a huge difference. When there is the possibility of a cancer diagnosis you will have to schedule several appointments. Every appointment I had was in a different location with a different scheduling service. Trying to fit everything in while doing my research and trying to come to some very important decisions can be overwhelming. I relied on my wife to make a lot of the calls and she did it without any hesitation. I could hear the frustration in her voice as she navigated the process. I hate that she had to put up with this, but I am so thankful that she did. I am not all that sure that I could have been as patient and kind as she was.

Not only did I rely on my wife, but I also had two excellent doctors. I never felt like my family physician or my urologist were watching the clock thinking about their next appointment. Nowadays a physician's schedule is often packed to the brim, not allowing for the one on one time needed deal with their patient. Being your own advocate means finding a doctor who does not live by a stopwatch. Don't forget to offer your doctor a little grace. You will not be their only patient, and you probably will not be their sickest patient. My Urologist was very upset when I told her that the biopsy results had come to my phone, and I knew what she was going to tell me. I told her that it was OK, it wasn't her fault that I ended up telling myself I had cancer, and that what was really important was how we were going to move forward.

I kept my condition very close until I had made my decision as to what course of treatment I was going to pursue. Some people will tell you about a relative they know who had prostate cancer. Their love and support is genuine and I am so thankful for the ones who offered me advice. The issue is that most of the advice you get comes to you second and third hand. They really don't know what the realities of prostate cancer are. They really don't understand how devastating the side effects of a treatment can be. Trying to make your best decision while being overwhelmed with well-meaning suggestions can make the decision very difficult. Keep your circle small and the path forward will be easier to find.

I had, and there is still a chance for reoccurrence, a very treatable form of cancer, but it is still cancer. Prostate cancer is just one of the cancers that show up at an increased incidence among firefighters. Female firefighters have their own issues on top of the other cancers firefighters must deal with. I was totally asymptomatic when I was diagnosed. As I have already said, you must be your own advocate. If your organization does not offer annual medical screening, use your own health insurance. Do not ignore the possibility of an occupational cancer and if there is any indication be aggressive in your approach.

Having cancer has been challenging, it has changed my life and is something that will stay in the back of my mind for the rest of my life. With all this being said the fire service is still in my mind the best job on the face of the earth. We must at times pay a price for being part of the service, but for me the rewards have been much more than the speed bump prostate cancer was.

TK12
PROBATIONARY
FIREFIGHTER
E12
TK12
ZELCH

ABOUT THE AUTHOR

Chief Dennis Reilly is a U.S. Army veteran of Operation Desert Storm and a 50-year fire service leader. He began his fire career in Cherry Hill, New Jersey, where he rose to the rank of Battalion Chief. After retiring, he transitioned into senior Chief Officer roles across the country, serving in Kansas, Missouri, North Carolina, and California. From combat zones to command posts, Reilly has lived a life of disciplined service and high-impact leadership.

Now retired, Chief Reilly owns *The First Line Fire Service Training Company, LLC*, where he delivers intensive, mission-focused training built around cultural transformation, operational accountability, and frontline leadership. Departments nationwide seek his guidance to spark internal change and elevate their culture throughout the ranks.

Chief Reilly was a founding member of New Jersey Task Force 1, deploying to New York City during the 9/11 terrorist attacks, reinforcing his unwavering service to threats foreign and domestic. During the Global War on Terror, he served as a protective services contractor in Iraq and Afghanistan, protecting government clients and assets in high-threat environments.

He has conducted multi-day leadership and culture-building events for fire departments across the country—customized to the needs of each agency.

Reilly holds a Master of Public Administration from Penn State University and is a Chief Fire Officer (CFO) designee. A published author in *Firehouse Magazine*, *Fire Engineering Magazine*, and *From The Green Notebook*, writing on high-performance leadership across fire service, military, and executive settings. He's also a respected speaker, he has presented at national and regional events including FDIC (Indianapolis, IN), MAFFC (Atlanta, GA), Orlando Fire Conference (FL), LIFT (Baton Rouge, LA), Craft & Culture Fire Conference (Iowa City, IA), Monadnock Fire Conference (Troy, NH), and CountyFireTactics.com (Pensacola Beach, FL)

Chief Reilly speaks to those who lead when it matters most—when time is short, stakes are high, and failure is not an option. His message blends battle-tested wisdom with modern fire service challenges, making him a sought-after voice for departments ready to shift their mindset, build resilient teams, and lead with integrity. He and his wife Ann have been married for over 39 years, and he is a proud father of two and grandfather of three.

www.ingramcontent.com/pod-product-compliance
Lightning Source LLC
LaVergne TN
LVHW010902110826
845149LV00005B/1446

* 9 7 8 1 9 5 9 2 4 0 0 9 9 *